GEORGE WHITEFIELD CHADWICK
His Symphonic Works

By
Bill F. Faucett

Composers of North America Series, No. 19

The Scarecrow Press, Inc.
Lanham, Md. & London

SCARECROW PRESS, INC.

Published in the United States of America
by Scarecrow Press, Inc.
4720 Boston Way
Lanham, Maryland 20706

4 Pleydell Gardens, Folkestone
Kent CT20 2DN, England

British Cataloguing-in-Publication Information Available

Library of Congress Cataloging-in-Publication Data

Faucett, Bill F.
George Whitefield Chadwick : his symphonic works / by Bill F. Faucett
p. cm. — (Composers of North America ; no. 19)
Includes bibliographical references and index.
1. Chadwick, G. W. (George Whitefield), 1854–1931. Symphonies
I. Title. II. Series.
MT130.C38F38 1996 784.2'184'092—dc20 95-14501 CIP MN

ISBN 0-8108-3038-8 (cloth : alk. paper)

Printed in the United States of America

™ The paper used in this publication meets the minimum requirements of American National Standard for Information Sciences—Permanence of Paper for Printed Library Materials, ANSI Z39.48–1984.

Composers of North America

Series Editors: John Beckwith, Sam Dennison, William C. Loring, Jr., Margery M. Lowens, Martha Furman Schleifer

1. *William Wallace Gilchrist, 1846–1916: A Moving Force in the Musical Life of Philadelphia,* by Martha Furman Schleifer, 1985
2. *Energy and Individuality in the Art of Anna Huntington, Sculptor, and Amy Beach,* Composer, by Myrna G. Eden, 1987
3. *Ruth Crawford Seeger: Memoirs, Memories, Music,* by Matilda Gaume, 1986
4. *An American Romantic-Realist Abroad: Templeton Strong and His Music,* by William C. Loring Jr., 1995
5. *Elinor Remick Warren: Her Life and Her Music,* by Virginia Bortin, 1987
6. *Horatio Parker, 1863–1919: His Life, Music, and Ideas,* by William K. Kearns, 1990
7. *Frances McCollin: Her Life and Music,* by Annette Maria DiMedio, 1990
8. *Hard Trials: The Life and Music of Harry T. Burleigh,* by Anne Key Simpson, 1990
9. *He Heard America Singing: Arthur Farwell, Composer and Crusading Music Educator,* by Evelyn Davis Culbertson, 1992
10. *Follow Me: The Life and Music of R. Nathaniel Dett,* by Anne Key Simpson, 1993
11. *Normand Lockwood: His Life and Music,* by Kay Norton, 1993
12. *Ridin' Herd to Writing Symphonies: An Autobiography,* by Radie Britain, 1995
13. *Henry Holden Huss: An American Composer's Life,* by Gary A. Greene, 1995
14. *Frederick Shepherd Converse (1871–1940): His Life and Music,* by Robert J. Garofalo, 1994
15. *John Weinzweig and His Music: The Radical Romantic of Canada,* by Elaine Keillor, 1994
16. *Amy Beach and Her Chamber Music: Biography, Documents, Style,* by Jeanell Wise Brown, 1994
17. *Music of Many Means: Sketches and Essays on the Music of Robert Erickson,* by Robert Erickson and John MacKay, 1995
18. *Divine Song on the Northeast Frontier: Maine's Sacred Tunebooks, 1800–1830,* by Linda G. Davenport, 1996
19. *George Whitefield Chadwick: His Symphonic Works,* by Bill F. Faucett, 1996

To Julie and Billy

I wish to express special thanks
to the family and heirs of
George Whitefield Chadwick.

CONTENTS

Table of Figures		ix
Acknowledgments		xi
Preface		xv
Series Editors Foreword		xiii
Chapter 1	Biographical Sketch	1
Chapter 2	Introduction to the Symphonies	5
Chapter 3	Symphony [No. 1] in C Major, Op. 5	8
Chapter 4	Symphony No. 2 in B^b Major, Op. 21	34
Chapter 5	Symphony in F (No. 3)	60
Chapter 6	Introduction to the Quasi-Symphonies	87
Chapter 7	*Symphonic Sketches*	89
Chapter 8	*Sinfonietta in D Major*	116
Chapter 9	*Suite Symphonique in E^b Major*	138
Chapter 10	Conclusion	160
Notes		171
Appendix I	The Complete Works of George Whitefield Chadwick	177
	Instrumental Music	
	Stage Works	
	Choral Music	
	Solo Songs	
Appendix II	Selected Performances of the Symphonic Works of George Whitefield Chadwick	195
Selected Discography		201
Selected Bibliography		203
Index		211
About the Author		215

TABLE OF FIGURES

Figure 1.	Program of Premiere Performance of Symphony [No. 1] in C Major, op. 5	10
Figure 2.	Title page, Symphony No. 2 in B^{b} Major, op. 21	35
Figure 3.	Title page, *Suite Symphonique*	139

ACKNOWLEDGMENTS

I am grateful to the many people who assisted me in the preparation of this volume. Most especially I wish to thank Dr. Douglass Seaton for his guidance and inspiration not only during this project, but over the course of my entire academic career.

Very special thanks to the members of my doctoral committee, each of whom lent considerable time and energy to this work in its early stages: Dr. Jeffery T. Kite-Powell, Dr. Bentley Shellahammer, and Dr. John Drew.

Dr. William C. Loring, my editor at Scarecrow Press, provided guidance and valuable advice during the many months we worked together. Without his insight and patience, this book would not have been possible.

Special acknowledgment is due Victor Fell Yellin, Chadwick's biographer, who was always eager to respond to my many inquiries about the composer, and openly shared the fruits of his lifetime of research on American music.

I am indebted to Steven Ledbetter, who generously provided me with information and commercially unavailable recordings of Chadwick's compositions. His unpublished *Sourcebook* (1983), a tremendously important tool for Chadwick research, provided much information about the reception history of the symphonic works and forms the basis of the "Complete Works" section of this monograph.

Dale Hudson, head music librarian at Florida State University (retired), was always willing to share information, often sending me an elusive program note or article.

Sincere thanks to Wayne D. Shirley, music specialist, Library of Congress; Diane Ota, curator of music, Boston Public Library; George Boziwick, curator, American Music Collection, The New York Library for the Performing Arts; Natalie Palme, librarian, The Harvard Musical Association; Jean A. Morrow, director of libraries, New England Conservatory of Music; Mary E. Rame,

Sibley Music Library, Eastman School of Music; Mary Elizabeth VandenBerge, manager, music department, Free Library of Philadelphia; Bill Coakle, for his assistance with the preparation of musical examples of the First Symphony; Linda L. Acosta, Saint Louis Symphony Orchestra; Timothy Flynn, Chicago Symphony Orchestra; Orrin Howard and Kimberly Barncastle, Los Angeles Philharmonic; Julie Eugenio, Philadelphia Orchestra; Peter Conover, Houston Symphony Orchestra; Patrick McGinn, Milwaukee Symphony Orchestra; Jane L. Terr, Indianapolis Symphony Orchestra; Steve Astle, San Francisco Symphony; Nick Jones, Atlanta Symphony Orchestra; John C. Loomans, Detroit Symphony Orchestra; and Ingrid Nelson, The Minnesota Orchestra.

Finally, I wish to thank my wife, Julie, for her assistance, support, and patience during the several years I worked on this project.

FOREWORD

The Series on Composers of North America is designed to focus attention on the development of art music and folk music from colonial times to the present. Few composers of art music before 1975 had their works performed frequently during their lifetime. Many suffered undeserved neglect.

Each volume consists of a substantial essay about the composer and a complete catalog of compositions, published and unpublished. Part I deals with the composer's life and works in the context of the artistic thought and the musical world of his or her time. In Part II the goals of the composer and critical comments by contemporaries are included, as are illustrations and musical examples. Some works which merit performance today are singled out for analysis and discussion. In Part III the catalog of the composer's output has full publication details, and locations of unpublished works are given. We hope that this series will make readers conscious and appreciative of our North American musical heritage.

The books are also intended to help performers and teachers seeking works to use. For them we designed the Part III catalog of the composer's music to allow a quick search for works the author finds of historic or current interest that may be considered for readings and hearings.

Series Editors:

John Beckwith, Sam Dennison, William C. Loring, Jr., Margery M. Lowens, Martha Furman Schleifer

PREFACE

By the early 1880s America was well on its way to establishing a strong tradition of orchestral performance. Although the nation was still relatively young and had only recently begun to forge its own musical identity, it benefited greatly from the many gifted musicians, both amateur and professional, who had emigrated from Europe. Musical activity flourished under their leadership through many music societies, clubs, and various types of organizations that introduced and maintained symphonic events in local communities long before the establishment of a professional symphony orchestra in the United States.

Instrumental musical undertakings in nineteenth-century America were concentrated primarily in the northeastern section of the country, most notably in New York City and Boston. New York City was far ahead of the nation when it founded its Philharmonic in 1842, and its official start had even been preceded by several distinguished philharmonic societies that made important contributions to the city's cultural life.

The Boston Symphony Orchestra was not founded until 1881, but it was similarly preceded by a number of important organizations. Orchestral activities occurred in the city as early as the late 1790s, and the Handel and Haydn Society, an important and still-flourishing music organization, was established in 1815. Groups such as the Musical Fund Society and the Harvard Musical Association had also played a vital role in developing the city's affection for orchestral music.

America's most important symphonic organizations were largely comprised of foreign musicians and directed by foreign conductors. Needless to say, their repertoires tended not to extend much beyond the oeuvre of the European masters whose works are still performed today; the nineteenth-century orchestras were, after all, paving the way for today's "standard" repertoire. Perhaps the degree to which conductors were forced to abide by the conventions of programming known compositions is nowhere better demonstrated than in the case of Theodore Thomas (1835–1905). German-born but raised in the United States, Thomas was at least as competent an impresario as he was a conductor. Having achieved success as a violinist, he went on to direct a number of orchestras during his lifetime; his longest tenure occurred with the New York Philharmonic, which he led from 1879 to 1891. Thomas's programs did little to enhance the position of American composers, as he could not risk the alienation of patrons, who were more interested in hearing accepted masterworks than new American works. Thomas's repertoire heavily favored compositions by Beethoven, Schubert, Schumann, Wagner, Brahms, and composers of similar stature. This bias toward European composition was a circumstance with which every music director and American composer had to contend, but it was all the more difficult to understand in light of the fact that Thomas was, in many respects and by all but birth, an American, and certainly the most prominent and gifted conductor who had been reared on American soil.

American composers, particularly those who relied on large ensembles to perform their works, often had some difficulty in getting them performed. Not only did they have to impress conductors with the quality of their works, but they suffered by constant comparison with the great masters already mentioned. Despite these difficulties, American composers were by no means completely denied hearings of their works.

Three early symphonic composers who worked in the United States in the period prior to the Civil War were able to secure performances of their works and made notable contributions to orchestral literature. Anthony Philip Heinrich (1781–1861), who had emigrated to the United States from Bohemia while in his twenties, was one of the first composers in America to work in the larger forms. He is noted more often for his eccentric nature than his compositions, and he tended to write works that elicit excitement as much from their descriptive titles as anything else. One of his more fanciful achievements is elaborately entitled *The Ornithological Combat of Kings; or, The Condor of the Andes and the Eagle of the Cordilleras*.

William Henry Fry (1813–1864) and George F. Bristow (1825–1898) both wrote a number of works for orchestra and were considered competent composers in their day, although their works exhibit little in the way of original thought. Fry's four symphonies bear programmatic titles, such as *Santa Claus* and *A Day in the Country,* and are somewhat simplistic in their use of musical materials, relying primarily on pleasing melodies, regular metrical patterns, and rudimentary harmony. Bristow's symphonic works achieve a depth and seriousness that few of his contemporaries were able to match, and although his craftsmanship was laudable, his compositions sound decidedly derivative of European influences. Like Heinrich, Fry and Bristow forged no lasting influence and have been almost completely forgotten by all but the scholarly community.

The first great American composer of symphonic works was John Knowles Paine (1839–1906). Paine composed only two symphonies, in 1875 and 1879, but his mastery of the genre is clear. His works sound very similar to those of the German masters with whom he had studied, both works are well-crafted, and the Second Symphony ("Im Frühling") is wonderfully imaginative. It must be noted that the very fact that his symphonies sounded German helped him to achieve critical acclaim from a New England press and musical public that regarded the late-Classic and early-Romantic symphonic aesthetic as the goal toward which every composer should strive.

Such was the condition of symphonic music in America when George Whitefield Chadwick emerged as a professional composer. When he returned to the United States after a period of study in Europe, he had already begun his First Symphony, and had thus embarked on one of the most important musical careers in the United States. Like John Knowles Paine, he had begun to garner the respect of musicians, conductors, and the press, and had helped the cause of American composition by making American works acceptable in the concert hall. But whereas Paine's works, while well-crafted and inventive, were clearly based upon accepted models, Chadwick began his symphonic career by emulating the masters but went on to create a style that was completely personal and completely American.

This book is intended to shed light on Chadwick's six symphonic works, that is, those multi-movement works for orchestra that were either conceived as wholes or composed as disparate movements and then compiled for performance and eventual publication. A brief biographical sketch introduces the highlights of the composer's life. Chapters are dedicated to the examination of each of the symphonic works, and topics discussed include their history, analysis, and critical reception.

The histories of the symphonic works are often problematic, because Chadwick spent very little time detailing the genesis of his compositions; nevertheless, what is known is chronicled here.

Analyses of the compositions are provided with the hope of imparting to the reader a detailed sense of Chadwick's personal symphonic style; numerous musical examples and analytical charts (based on language presented in Jan LaRue's *Guidelines for Style Analysis*) are included to help achieve this objective. The composer's musical language displays a clear command of form, harmony, rhythm, texture, and, above all, orchestration. Fortunately, his rigorous German conservatory training did not, as it did in the case of many young American composers, rob him of his humor and imagination. Neither did Chadwick look solely to his German predecessors for inspiration; he was clearly aware of and admired modern French currents in music.

Chadwick was aware of the most important aspect of musical life in his times, the concern about "Americanism," but seems not to have been very interested in it. He knew of Dvořák's statements with respect to the potential of Negro or American Indian music forming a basis for American music, but Chadwick felt strongly about employing his own brand of Americanism rather than resorting to what he must have considered uncomfortable artifice.

That is not to say that Chadwick was not influenced by some elements of these musics, especially Negro music, but he tended not to use the melodic materials of these cultures. Chadwick's Americanism included the employment of traditional forms and harmonies in conjunction with the use of syncopated rhythms of Afro-Caribbean or even ragtime origin; pleasing, folksonglike melodies of a Scotch-Irish, sometimes pentatonic, cast; bold, colorful orchestration that includes a good deal of reliance on the winds and percussion; and a lively sense of humor that might parody Debussy or give a Bach melody to the xylophone.

The critical reception of Chadwick's works provides insight about many aspects of the composer, his music, and his work as a conductor. Some of the most important historical information about the symphonic works comes from well-researched newspaper columns, and the reader is treated to a variety of opinions, informed and uninformed, about the music itself. While a few reviews reveal little more than how the critic felt about a given work, most are impressively convincing and highly technical in their analysis. Chadwick's love of conducting and the impact that it had on the success of his symphonic compositions is also investigated.

Finally, two appendices are included, the second of which lists selected performances of the symphonic works by major orchestras in the United States from the works' premieres to the present. The first appendix is a complete roster of Chadwick's compositions. Hopefully, the bibliography and discography will lead to further investigations into the life and music of this important and extremely talented composer.

CHAPTER 1

BIOGRAPHICAL SKETCH

George Whitefield Chadwick was born on November 13, 1854 in the town of Lowell, Massachusetts.[1] Although composers of the Second New England School are often stereotyped as belonging to a privileged class, Chadwick was born to a working-class family. His parents, both singers, were competent enough to participate in local singing groups, and his older brother, Fitts Henry, probably gave the talented young George his first music lessons. By the time Chadwick was fifteen he was playing the organ well enough to maintain an active performance schedule in various churches in Lawrence, Massachusetts.[2]

Little is known about Chadwick's extramusical education; he provided no indication that he was in any way a scholar. On the contrary, he dropped out of high school in 1871 to go to work for his father, a former carpenter who had since become an insurance broker. The following year, Chadwick began piano lessons with local pedagogue Carlyle Petersilea (1844–1903), a former student of Carl Reinecke (1824–1910) and Ignaz Moscheles (1794–1870). During these early student years the young musician also took lessons with organists Eugene Thayer (1838–1889) and Dudley Buck (1839–1909), the latter of whom had studied in Leipzig. In 1872 Chadwick began to emerge as a serious musician; he entered the New England Conservatory as a special student. While there, he had the opportunity to study organ with renowned organist George E. Whiting (1840–1923) and harmony with Stephen A. Emery (1841–1891), another product of a Leipzig education.

Having completed a course of study at the Conservatory, although without the benefit of an academic degree, Chadwick secured his first teaching position in 1876. With a hearty recommendation from Theodore Presser (1848–1925), himself a very competent musician and later an important publisher, Chadwick went to work in the music department of Olivet College in Olivet, Michigan.[3] There he taught courses in harmony, counterpoint, form, and composition, as well as applied music on various instruments and voice. Even though the position gave him a fine opportunity to hone his skills as a professional, he decided to leave the United States for study abroad during his first academic year at Olivet.

Upon Chadwick's arrival in Europe in 1877 he went directly to Berlin to study with Karl August Haupt (1810–1891). According to Chadwick's biographer Victor Fell Yellin, Haupt, whose reputation was based on his skill as an organist, was "not prepared to instruct him in composition and orchestration."[4] Upon discovering this, Chadwick left immediately for Leipzig, where he began a close personal and musical relationship with Salomon Jadassohn (1831–1902), a student of Liszt. Jadassohn proved to be one of Chadwick's best-loved and most influential teachers. The master was noted for his rigorous methods and conservative tastes. Additionally, Chadwick had the opportunity to study with Carl Reinecke, the conductor of the Leipzig Gewandhaus Orchestra and an extremely competent composer and teacher.[5]

In 1879 Chadwick began a journey through Germany and France with a roving band of artists, mostly painters, who were known as the "Duveneck Boys," so named for the group's mentor, Frank Duveneck (1848–1919), an accomplished painter in his own right.[6] This brief sojourn had a lasting impact on the impressionable young Chadwick and left him with a lifelong love of all French art. Chadwick so loved France that he gave thought to the possibility of studying with César Franck in Paris. Later he changed his mind and moved to Munich, where he began organ and composition studies with Josef Rheinberger at the Hochschule für Musik.[7] Bomberger has noted that although Chadwick studied with Rheinberger for only a brief period, he must have been impressed with the master's methods. Chadwick sent many of his most promising students to Munich to study with Rheinberger, including Horatio Parker.[8]

The skills and techniques that Chadwick developed during his years in Germany were highly profitable. Yellin writes that

> In teaching those fundamentals of form that exist irrespective of personal style or correct fashion, conservative peda-

> gogues such as Jadassohn, Reinecke, and Rheinberger gave Chadwick the tools with which he could craft his own kind of music.[9]

Chadwick returned to Boston in 1880 and began his new career as a private teacher and organist.[10] It was also during this period, the early 1880s, that Chadwick began to compose regularly and in earnest. The importance of his works was increasingly realized by critics, and the Boston premiere of his *Rip Van Winkle* Overture precipitated a steady stream of performances in and around the city.[11] In spring 1882 Chadwick accepted a teaching position in harmony and composition at the New England Conservatory and began what would be a 40-year relationship with that institution.[12] He became its director in 1897, a post he held until 1930.[13] As director, Chadwick emphasized rigorous courses not unlike those he had taken as a student in Germany, with a curriculum that included harmony, counterpoint, orchestration, and composition. He also introduced a large and varied repertoire to the conservatory orchestra, which he conducted, and developed an opera workshop, the first in the United States.[14]

Chadwick's talents as a conductor are often overlooked, but it seems clear that he harbored the desire to conduct professionally.[15] He frequently conducted his own works with various organizations, including the Harvard Musical Association and the Boston Symphony Orchestra. Early in his career he held the post of director and conductor of the Springfield Festival (1890–1899) and the Worcester Festival (1897–1901), in addition to his duties as conductor of the New England Conservatory orchestra. As director of these ensembles Chadwick conducted a variety of compositions, including Berlioz's *Le damnation de Faust,* Franck's *Les beatitudes,* Brahms's *Ein deutsches Requiem,* MacDowell's *Lancelot and Elaine,* Verdi's *Te Deum,* and various works by Louis Aubert, Emmanuel Chabrier, Arthur Shepherd, and Edward Burlingame Hill.[16]

It was in his roles as a composer and music educator that Chadwick had his most enduring successes. As composer, Chadwick was prolific; his oeuvre includes seven works for stage (including operas and operettas), six symphonies, five overtures, several works variously labeled "symphonic poem," "symphonic fantasy," and "symphonic drama," and other assorted works for orchestra, including marches and occasional pieces. In addition, he composed no fewer than 21 works for chorus and orchestra, and a number of pieces for solo voice and orchestra. Chadwick's smaller-scale music includes over 100 compositions (sacred and secular) for chorus, 10 instrumental chamber works, including five string quartets, nearly 150 solo songs, and assorted works for piano and organ. It is worth mentioning that the noted critic W.S.B. Mathews once wrote that the much-acclaimed American baritone David Bispham considered Chadwick "one of the greatest songwriters in the world."[17] Two notable omissions from Chadwick's works list are concertos and instrumental solo sonatas. There is no clear answer as to why Chadwick neglected to compose in these genres; one possible reason may be that his own inability, or perhaps disinterest, in mastering the keyboard dissuaded him from attempting to compose virtuoso works for a single instrument.

Chadwick's career as an educator was also enviable. Not only did his textbook *Harmony: A Course of Study* reach an impressive audience (through 74 editions), but his roster of students reads like a *Who's Who* of American music in the final decades of the nineteenth century and the first three decades of the twentieth.[18] Chadwick students included Horatio Parker, Frederick Shepherd Converse, Edward Burlingame Hill, Arthur Farwell, Daniel Gregory Mason, and William Grant Still, among many others.[19]

In addition to having taught many of the best composers in America, by the end of his life Chadwick had accumulated numerous honors and awards, including honorary degrees from Yale University (A.M., 1897) and Tufts University (Ll.D., 1905). He was also elected to the American Academy of Arts and Letters and the National Institute of Arts and Letters, the latter having awarded Chadwick its Gold Medal in 1928.

By the beginning of World War I, Chadwick was regarded as "old hat" by younger composers.[20] The style of composition in which he had worked throughout his career was fast being superseded by various modernisms, including atonality, impressionism, and even jazz. By his final year, 1931, Chadwick had witnessed his own decline into relative obscurity, his importance relegated to the history books, and his music suffering from near-total neglect.

CHAPTER 2

INTRODUCTION TO THE SYMPHONIES

Of Chadwick's six symphonies, only three are actually titled "symphony." Chadwick composed these three works in 1877–1881, 1883–1885, and 1893, respectively. Although they are closely related to compositions from the great tradition of nineteenth-century conservative symphonic style, the works are often strikingly original. Early in his career Chadwick embraced the classically trained, early-Romantic school of composition identified first with Mendelssohn and Schumann and later with Brahms and Dvořák. The influence of these masters can readily be discovered in his first three symphonies.

The reason for Chadwick's initial venture into the composition of a symphony is easy to discern. In Leipzig he was surrounded by the memory of all of the notable symphonists who had made that city famous; to compose for orchestra in the shadow of those masters must have been an exhilarating experience for the young Yankee. It is also noteworthy that one of his teachers, Carl Reinecke, led the famous Leipzig Gewandhaus Orchestra, bearers of the heritage of Mendelssohn, and that the towering figure of German symphonic music in the 1870s, Johannes Brahms, often visited the city. An eager student such as Chadwick probably could hardly wait to start composing for the large ensemble.

The situation regarding composition was vastly different in America from that in the inspiring Leipzig. It would have been a tremendous challenge to any young composer to undertake the task of composing a symphony in the United States during the post-Civil War era. Although Boston, one of the young nation's most cosmopolitan cities, regularly heard performances of the accepted orchestral masterpieces, symphonies by native composers were still somewhat unusual. John Knowles Paine (1839–1906) was among the first to introduce audiences to symphonies by American composers with his Symphonies No. 1 (1876) and No. 2 (1880), and the success that he achieved with these works cannot be underestimated.[1] Nevertheless, the door was by no means completely open to young American musicians who hoped to carve for themselves a career in music. They could only aspire to the grand expectations of the largely German-trained conductors and critics, not to mention audiences who had been groomed to adhere to European standards of taste. In his well-known article of 1915, "The American Composer," Henry F. Gilbert addressed part of the problem, writing,

> The American composer, even one of the best and most earnest sort, in submitting a composition of his to one of our European-American symphony-orchestra conductors, must abide by his decision respecting its worthiness of performance. The decision of the orchestral conductor respecting the value of the work submitted is naturally influenced by the degree in which the new work approaches those great European models with which his life-training has made him familiar.[2]

Chadwick and his colleagues were compelled by a variety of reasons to compose in a rather restrained style. Not the least of these was the simple fact that they had been raised in a Puritan environment. In a discussion of the music of several New England composers, including Chadwick and a number of his contemporaries, musicologist Nicholas Tawa notes the generally conservative approach to composition that American musicians often embraced:

> True to their New England inheritance, the composers disciplined themselves against excessive individuality and temperamental excess. Firm convictions, consistently held, guided their thinking. They set themselves the task of balancing the ear's desire for sensuous sound-colors, the mind's demand for rational forms, and the imagination's inclination toward unexpected and random fancies. Music's beauty to them resided in achieving an equilibrium among all three.[3]

Tawa's words apply well to Chadwick's First Symphony. In instrumentation, form, rhythm, texture, and melody, it is obviously an early work, one in which the composer was just beginning to explore his craft. Chadwick's Second and Third Symphonies, while still based on traditional symphonic thought, show substantial advancement over the First. Not only did the composer experiment with pentatonicism and other exotic techniques borrowed from impressionism and other progressive styles, but these later symphonies display much greater facility with rhythm and harmony, a keen sense for orchestration, and a more imaginative overall conception.

CHAPTER 3

SYMPHONY [NO. 1] IN C MAJOR, OP. 5

HISTORY

Chadwick began his Symphony No. 1, op. 5, in 1877, while he was studying composition with Jadassohn and Reinecke in Leipzig.[1] Sketches for the composition were prepared during the next several years, particularly while Chadwick was in Dresden and Switzerland, where he seems to have enjoyed a fruitful period. The first movement was completed in Munich in early 1880, during the brief period that Chadwick was under the tutelage of Rheinberger. The rest of the First Symphony was taken up after Chadwick's return to Boston and was completed on November 23, 1881.

The work is clearly a student piece, adhering to accepted rules and standards of conservative compositional practice. It does, however, display several traits that prove significant to later developments in his style. It should be noted that this was neither Chadwick's first effort at writing for orchestra nor his first effort in the symphonic style, that is, in treating material in a developmental fashion. Of the four works that preceded opus 5, two are string quartets, both of which display a remarkable command of developmental technique. One critic noted that the Second Quartet is "fresh and pregnant in themes, musician-like in treatment [i.e., developmental], original and yet free from extravagance, and full of spirit and legitimate effect".[2]

Another predecessor of the First Symphony, Chadwick's *Rip Van Winkle* Overture, completed in 1879, is scored for the same forces that he used in his first two symphonies. The review of *Rip Van Winkle* in *Dwight's Journal of Music* deserves some attention. In it, the reviewer (presumably Dwight) noted that several stylistic influences were, to his thinking, unexpectedly missing from the work. He wrote that the overture included

> none of those traits of Wagnerism which some have felt themselves called upon to find in his scoring; the brass, to be sure, is freely used, only richly, never overpoweringly. The whole piece is certainly effective, and more than merely pleasing. If it have [*sic*] no very marked, decided originality, it betrays no slavish imitation; it is uncommonly free of Mendelssohnian echos. . . .[3]

In fact, Chadwick's symphonies are often paradoxical; sometimes they are very original, exhibiting traits that are decidedly the work of an extraordinarily talented composer. At other times they are "slavish imitations," and not always good ones. But as reviewers throughout Chadwick's career were to write, he was a sturdy craftsman, whose works were, more often than not, "effective, and more than merely pleasing."

When considering Chadwick's First Symphony, one must also consider the long shadow cast by John Knowles Paine (1839–1906), the leading composer in the United States during the period in which Chadwick's symphony was composed. Paine had built an enviable career in music; his record of success in composition and teaching was tremendous and he was the first musician to achieve the rank of full professor at an American university, one no less prestigious than Harvard, in 1875.[4] Indeed, it is very possible that when Chadwick returned to New England from his European sojourn, Paine's career was the model upon which he sought to develop his own.

In the genre of the symphony, Paine's two compositions are the first major achievements by an American (although they are by no means the first such compositions attempted by an American). His Symphony No. 1 in C minor, op. 23, was premiered in Boston on January 26, 1876 by the Theodore Thomas Orchestra, while the better-known Symphony No. 2 in A major, op. 34 ("Im Frühling") was premiered on March 10, 1880 by the Boston Philharmonic, followed the next day by a performance by the Harvard Musical Association.[5] Although we are not certain whether Chadwick attended the premiere of Paine's First Symphony, it is reasonable to suggest that the young composer, newly returned from European study and causing quite a stir himself, attended at least one of the presentations of Paine's Second Symphony. It is also reasonable to suggest

Harvard Musical Association.

Fourth Symphony Concert

(SEVENTEENTH SEASON)

AT THE

BOSTON MUSEUM,

Thursday Afternoon, Feb. 23, 1882,

AT 3 O'CLOCK PRECISELY.

Conductor . . CARL ZERRAHN.

Violin Leader . BERNHARD LISTEMANN.

Figure 1. Program of Premiere Performance of Symphony [No. 1] in C major, op.5

PROGRAMME.

---

1. OVERTURE: "The Water-carrier" . . . CHERUBINI

2. DUET: "Sull' aria," from "Le Nozze di Figaro" MOZART

   MRS. E. HUMPHREY ALLEN and
   MISS MARGUERITE HALL.

3. SYMPHONY in C (MS., first performance) G. W. CHADWICK

   Allegro molto e sostenuto.—Presto.
   Scherzo: Allegro molto vivace.
   Adagio espressivo.
   Finale: Introduction.—Allegro molto.—Presto.

4. DUET from "Beatrice et Benedict" . . . . BERLIOZ

   (First time in Boston.)

   MRS. E. HUMPHREY ALLEN and
   MISS MARGUERITE HALL.

5. OVERTURE to "William Tell" . . . . . ROSSINI

FIFTH (LAST) CONCERT ON THURSDAY AFTERNOON, MARCH 9.

Fourth Symphony in D minor, *Schumann;* Piano Concerto in G, *Beethoven* (by request), Prof. CARL BAERMANN, of Munich; Serenade in D, for String Orchestra (first time), *Fuchs;* Piano-forte Solos; Overture to "Ruy Blas," *Mendelssohn.*

that, early on in his career as a symphonist, Chadwick was familiar with both of Paine's compositions. After all, as Nicholas Tawa has noted, many of the Boston composers knew one another and regularly gathered for discussions about music and other topics.[6]

Chadwick's knowledge of Paine's work is further corroborated by the fact that the younger Yankee composer wrote glowingly of his elder's efforts. Chadwick wrote that Paine's First Symphony gave its composer recognition as a romantic composer "of high ideals and genuine imagination." He also stated that Paine's work in the genre encouraged younger composers to write symphonies that, at the time, had few American practitioners.[7]

Given the lengthy germination period of the first movement of Chadwick's First Symphony and the rapidity with which it was completed following his return to Boston, it seems likely that Paine's success in symphonic composition may have encouraged Chadwick to complete the work he had begun several years earlier. While there is little resemblance between Paine's two symphonies and Chadwick's first, other than their generally conservative nature and high-quality craftsmanship, there is little doubt but that Chadwick was affected by the older master, psychologically if not compositionally.

There is no record of a performance of the First Symphony since its premiere by the Harvard Musical Association on February 23, 1882. That single presentation was conducted by the composer. The dedication, to his stepmother, reveals the esteem in which the young Chadwick held his father's wife:

> To her, whose tender, faithful affection, no natural parent could have exceeded, whose steadfast love has been a talisman, and whose prayers a guiding star, through many stormy years of trial and temptation, this work is most gratefully dedicated by her affectionate son.

ANALYSIS

Movement 1

The first movement of the C-major Symphony is cast in a well-articulated sonata form (see Diagram 1–1).

Diagram 1–1. Formal Structure of First Movement.

		Part 1 Section 1					
Theme:	Intro.	P		(P)	(P)		(P)
Keys:	C:V	I	V	I	IV	V	ii
MM.:	1–4	5	12	21	29	37	41
Comment:	$\frac{3}{4}$			horns	frags.		

Theme:					
Key:	I	V	(a-g-f#-f-e)	B maj.	I
MM.:	45	52	53	57	59
Comment:			desc. fig.		hem.

						Part 1 Section 2
Theme:	P		t			S
Key:	V	I	g:	Aug^6	B (V/e)	e:i
MM.:	61	65	69	76	77	80
Comment:	dotted rhythm		new idea			

Theme:	(S)					(S)			t
Key:	i	(b—D)			C:V^7	I	iii^6_4		
MM.:	89	92	96	97	104	105	109	112	113
Comment:				ped.					

Theme:	(S)							
Key:		i	a	vii^{o7}/D	C:V^6_5/V	V^7/V	V	V^9/a
MM.:	115	117	123	127	133	136	143	148
Comment:	frags.		dotted rhythms					

		Part 2 Section 3								
Theme:		(S)		t						
Key:	a	C:V^6_4	V	I	G:v^7	V^7	I	V^7	I	I
MM.:	149	153	160	161	165	171	173	179	181	189
Comment:		vln.					Chad. trans.		hem.	

Theme:					P				
Key:	B	B	vii^{o4}_{3}/C	Aug^6	E:I	A:I	V	g:V^7	V
MM.:	193	197	201	208	209	213	214	217	220
Comment:		frags.			horn	frags.		bass	ww.

Theme:						t				
Key:	g	C:V-I	F:V^4_2	I^6	I	E^b:I^6	V^7	I^6	IV	IV
MM.:	221	224	226	227	231	234	235	241	249	251
Comment:										

Theme:		(P)			S				
Key:	g:$ii^{ø7}$	i	V	Aug^6	V	i			
MM.:	253	257	261	268	269	273	281	285	289
Comment:						fugato vln. II\cel.\bass\ww			

Theme:		P	S						
Key:	V^7/B^b:I			G-G#-A-B^b-B-C		V/E^b:I		I	f
MM.:	296	297	309	313	318	320	321	325	329
Comment:	horn			ascent			Chad. trans.		

Theme:	P					(S)		
Key:	F#:I^6_4	Aug^6	A:I^6_4	$vii^{ø6}_{5}$/V	i^6	C:V^7/V	I^6_4	IV
MM.:	337	344	345	349	350	352	353	361
Comment:								

Part 2

Section 4

Theme:				P						P
Key:	V^4_3/V	I^6_4	V	I	V/V	V	IV	V	IV	V/c:i
MM.:	368	369	377	385	391	392	393	397	399	401
Comment:										horns

Theme:							(P)				
Key:	i^6	V	i	V^6_4/vi	vi	ii	ii	i^6	ii	Aug^6	a:V
MM.:	405	411	412	418	419	421	423	425	429	432	433
Comment:											

Theme:		S				S			S
Key:	Aug^6	i	C:V^7	I	V^7/A	a	C:V/V	V^7	I
MM.:	436	437	441	442	444	445	450	452	460
Comment:								pedal	

Theme:			S						N	
Key:	a:i	iv	i	C:V	I	I	ii	vii^{ø7}/V	V	I^6
MM.:	469	471	473	476	477	478	479	483	489	493
Comment:			dotted rhythm						vln.I	

Theme:	P								
Key:	vii$^{ø4}_{2}$/f	iv	ii	V	I^6	IV	I^6	V^7	I
MM.:	501	502	505	509	513	517	525	527	529
Comment:	inversion								

	Coda Section 1						
Theme:	P		t				P
Key:	I	I	I	I^6	I^6	I	Aug^6
MM.:	537	541–545		550	553	557	564
Comment:	inv.						

Theme:		P	P				t
Key:	V/ii	ii$^6_4$	V	I$^6_4$	IV	V/V	V$^4_2$/A^b:
MM.:	565	569	573	577	581	585	589
Comment:		oboe solo	bass		dotted rhythm		

Theme:						S					
Key:	I^6	I	IV	IV	ii^7/C:	I$^6_4$	I$^6_4$	vi	V/iii	V	V^7
MM.:	597	601	605	607	609	613	619	621	623	631–42	
Comment									hem.		

	Section 2							Section 3	
Theme:	P								
Key:	I	V	I$^6_4$	IV	vii^{ø7}/V	ii$^4_2$	vii^{ø7}/A	a	C:I$^6_4$
MM.:	643	647	659	663	665	666	669	670	671
Comment:	$\frac{6}{8}$ vivace							$\frac{4}{4}$	

								Section 4	
Theme:									
Key:	V^7	I	I_4^6	I_4^6	V/vi	I_4^6	V	I——	I
MM.:	682	683	687	689	691	699	702	703	715
Comment:								Presto	

The movement begins with a four-measure introduction, marked "Lento," on the dominant. The opening is a quiet, understated prelude to the exposition, which begins in measure 5. The theme that announces the principal tonal area (P), is stated in the first violin part. It is a simple melody and would seem somewhat studied were it not for its rhythmic vitality. The music begins with the hemiola that emphasizes the half-note value (meas. 5–6) and then moves on in the following measures to emphasize c^1, e^1, and c^2, also in half-note values. Simultaneously, this passage expresses a rhythmic figure that is important throughout the symphony and clearly outlines the tonality of the movement (Example 1).

Chadwick scored the work primarily for strings, relegating the winds and timpani to mostly accompanimental roles. Like the *Rip Van Winkle* Overture, this work does not display the traits of Mendelssohn or those of Wagner; it rather has a closer affinity to Beethoven. Here the brass is certainly not used "freely" or "richly," but only at points that call for added articulation. This is essentially true for the lower brass. The woodwind instruments are

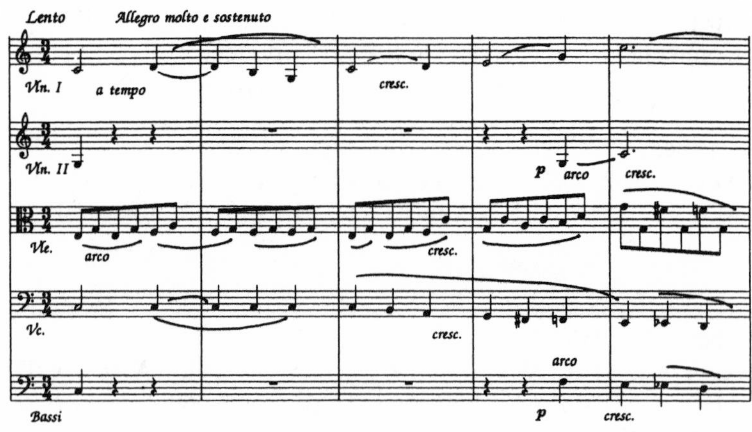

Example 1. Symphony in C, op. 5, mvt. 1, meas. 5–9.

employed somewhat more frequently in melodic roles, but are largely accompanimental. Chadwick often used the horns as part of the woodwind choir.

One expects little in the way of development in this section, and the passage simply states but does not exploit the material. Until the next main section arrives (meas. 82) there is a predominance of tonic and dominant harmonies, although a temporary move to the subdominant takes place in measure 29. The music progresses to the submediant at measure 53 before a descending bass line leads to a B-major harmony at measure 57. At this point comes the first appearance in the symphonies of what turns out to be a significant device in Chadwick's symphonic oeuvre: his use of simple transitions that employ primarily unison string or woodwind parts that lack harmonic underpinning (Example 2). These "Chadwickian" transition passages avoid the complex textures and harmonies that often accompany transitions in sonata forms from section to section or key to key and serve very effectively to delineate sections from one another.

The rhythmic shift that occurs during this transitional phrase, from compound meter in measures 57–58 to simple triple meter with hemiola in measures 59–60, causes considerable ambiguity by heightening the sense of instability in the transitional passage.

Section 2 is reached in measure 80. It is not, as one might expect in a student composition, in the dominant key, but rather in E

Example 2. Symphony in C, op. 5, mvt. 1, meas. 57–61.

minor, the dominant's relative minor. Precedents for the employment of the minor mode rather than the dominant at this point in a sonata form exist; Schumann had used a modulation from B-flat major to a secondary theme in D minor (meas. 81) in his Symphony No. 1 in B-flat major, op. 38 ("Spring") (1841). Brahms used a similar harmonic movement in his Symphony No. 2 in D major, op. 73 (1877); in the first movement of that composition the D-major opening leads to the secondary theme in F-sharp minor (meas. 82), while in the fourth movement the tonic opening progresses to the secondary theme in A minor (meas. 78).

While it is not completely certain that Chadwick knew these scores in his early years, one may be reasonably sure that he did. Schumann and Brahms had both been active in Leipzig, and Chadwick had heard the latter conduct the Leipzig premiere of his First Symphony.[8] Further, Brahms's Second Symphony was published in 1878, and was no doubt available to the young American composer for close study.

The tempo slows for the presentation of the theme associated with the secondary key(s) (Example 3).

The secondary theme, marked "espressivo," is a dolorous, somewhat static melody that stands in stark contrast to the vivacity of the primary theme. The present melody, played by the first violins, is accompanied by the lower woodwinds and the strings, which make for a very transparent texture. The thinness of this scoring, coupled with the frequent use of half steps, the narrow range of the melody, and the tempo, adds to the somber effect. The movement does not dwell on this theme, and by measure 113 the music is again in transition. At this point there is a brief moment of dialogue that uses the secondary theme as its source. It begins in the first clarinet part, then progresses to the viola and on to the first violins. A dotted-quarter/eighth-note rhythm in measure 119 prepares the appearance of a new dotted-rhythm figure in measure 123. This rhythm, used here for the first time in the work, lends the movement new vitality. It also provides more material that can be developed in the next section.

The most significant feature of the remainder of Section 2 is the abandonment of E minor and the alternation between C major and A minor to the end of the exposition. This creates even more ambiguity, for the music has undergone some development before the "development" section proper, and the impact of the develop-

Example 3. Symphony in C, op. 5, mvt. 1, meas. 88–96.

ment's arrival is lessened. The drama of sonata structure is undermined by the ambiguity of tonality before the development section.

Part 2/Section 3 first displays Chadwick's considerable interest in developmental procedures. The development section, which begins in measure 153, is by far the longest section of the movement, occupying 231 measures. Throughout, it displays Chadwick's command of standard thematic and harmonic resources, although there is little that seems particularly unexpected. Rapid harmonic shifts occur throughout, with some concentration on tonic and dominant, a somewhat unusual feature in the development of a sonata-form movement. There are several progressions into remote key areas, including B major (meas. 197), and E-flat major (meas. 234). No pattern may be easily discerned in the harmonic progressions in this section. The section employs well-established techniques associated with development style, including fugato (meas. 209), rhythmic destabilization by means of hemiola (meas. 321 and 369), and skillful manipulation of themes.

The music reaches Section 4 in measure 385, where C major returns with its original thematic material. Many previous ideas are recapitulated in this section, including the S theme in A minor (meas. 437) and C major (meas. 460). The dotted-rhythm figure appears in measure 473 (cf. meas. 123), and an important new countermelody joins in at measure 489.

The coda of this movement includes another feature that later became important to Chadwick's mature style. The composer had a penchant for employing multi-sectional codas in his works, each section of which may feature different styles from those previously sounded in the movement. Often new themes are introduced, as well. Frequently, these codas employ quick tempos and are "finalelike" in style. The addition of these long, rousing codas may be part of the reason that Chadwick came to be known, undoubtedly to his chagrin, as a composer of lighter works and orchestral showpieces.

The source of Chadwick's inspiration for the creation of multi-sectional codas is unclear. One possibility is that he borrowed the idea from Schumann, who had employed a similar coda in the fourth movement of his Fourth Symphony in 1851 ("Schneller" in meas. 188 and "Presto" in meas. 211). This is the only symphony in which Schumann clearly divided the coda into two parts; the first movement of the First Symphony also features a long coda, however. Although not marked off by a double bar, the coda of the first movement is multi-sectional.

The present coda includes four clearly articulated sections: Section 1 (meas. 537–642) is the most complex, with movement from C major through A-flat major (meas. 589), then back to C. Section 2 begins in measure 643 and presents the P theme in $\frac{6}{8}$ meter. Section 3, beginning in measure 670, moves from A minor to C major in $\frac{4}{4}$ meter. Here the music exploits a tonal juxtaposition that has already been noted in this composition (cf. meas. 113–153). Section 4, marked "Presto," is entirely in C major, beginning in measure 703.

Movement 2

The second movement of the First Symphony, a Scherzo in $\frac{3}{4}$ meter, is in the key of C minor (see Diagram 1–2).

Diagram 1–2. Formal Structure of Second Movement.

						Section 1					
Theme:	A					A					
Key:	c:i	III	i	V/V	V	V	iv^7—	iv^7	V	i	III
MM.:	1	5	9	15	16	17	18	30	34	35	38
Comment:	$\frac{3}{4}$										

										Section 2	
Theme:			A				A			B	
Key:	vii$^{o6}_{5}$/V	V	i	V	iv	V^7	i—	—i—	—Ab:	I	V
MM.:	42	57	58	62	66	72	78	94		98	101
Comment:										Trio	

Theme:			B				t		
Key:	I	I	I^6	V	V	I	c:vii^{o6}/V	Aug^6	i
MM.:	106	113	114	122	128	129	131	139	147
Comment:							$\frac{3}{4}$		

		Section 3									
Theme:		A				(A)					
Key:	i	i	III	i	V/V	iv	iv	iv	Aug^6	i^6	i$^6_4$
MM.:	151	163	167	171	177	179	187	197	203	206	210
Comment:											

Theme:	(A)					(A)
Key:	i	V	iv	V^7	i	V
MM.:	219	223	227	233	239	241
Comment:						

				Section 4			
Theme:				B			
Key:	i—	—i	V/F:	I	V	I—	—I
MM.:	243	255	258	259	266	267	274
Comment:						Trio	

								Section 5	
Theme:	(B)							A	
Key:	iii	V	V	vi	V	I	V^7/A	A	c:vii^6_5/V
MM.:	275	279—	—283	287	289	290	293	294	295
Comment:									

Theme:							
Key:	vi^{o6}_5		g:i	vi	V^7	c:i	B^b—B^b
MM.:	303	309–310	311	312	314	317	319–323
Comment:		silence					

						Coda					
Theme:						(A)					
Key:	V^6_5	i^6	iv	V^6_5/V	Aug^6	i	i	i	V^7	i—	—i
MM.:	327	330	334	335	337	343	351	380	389	393	394
Comment:											

The movement is cast in five-part rondo form with a coda. While the exact model upon which Chadwick based this composition is not known, the possible inspiration for the structure again may be Schumann or Brahms. The scherzo of Schumann's First Symphony (1841) is a five-part rondo with a multi-sectional coda, while the third movement ("Allegretto grazioso") of Brahms's Second Symphony (1877) employs the same general structural plan.

The first section presents the main scherzo theme in the first violins in the tonic key (Example 4).

Example 4. Symphony in C, op. 5, mvt. 2, meas. 1—9.

This pianissimo, understated theme outlines the C-minor triad in the first six measures. Marked staccato, the theme is balanced by a thinly textured countermelody in the second violin and viola parts. By measure 9 the strings are joined by the woodwinds, which also present the scherzo theme. In measure 18 the theme is sounded on the subdominant, where it remains for several bars, returning to the tonic minor in measure 35. The music remains in C minor for the remainder of the section, with fragments of the main theme sounding in measures 58 and 78, before a transition is reached in measure 94. The transition itself is rather unusual; following the cadence in the tonic, sustained Cs in the first and second horns, trumpets and timpani, are sounded against B flats in the violas and cellos. The harmony gives the impression of a dominant-seventh chord built on B flat as it progresses to the next section.

Section 2, marked "Trio" and in A-flat, is reached in measure 98. The duple-meter trio theme is a flowing, lilting melody, folk-like in character (Example 5). The smooth, symmetrical phrasing of the theme, coupled with the slowed tempo, simple harmonization, and relaxed rhythmic activity, produces the impression of folksong.

The scherzo theme returns in Section 3 in measure 163. As in Section 1, there is brief movement to the subdominant, but the section remains primarily on the tonic. The remainder of Section 3 is devoted to the manipulation of motives derived from the main theme. The section ends on the dominant of F.

Section 4, in F major, is reached in measure 259, and the B theme sounds. Unlike the previous (A-flat) presentation of the B section, this section is somewhat more harmonically elaborate, employing mediant and submediant harmonies at important points (meas. 275, 278, 287).

Example 5. Symphony in C, op. 5, mvt. 2, meas. 98–105.

Section 5 begins with the return of the scherzo theme in measure 295. While this final statement of the theme is the most harmonically elaborate section of the movement, passing through B-flat major and G minor, the music is still somewhat conservative. One of the most interesting segments of this part is the startling dominant harmony at measure 335, followed by several augmented-sixth chords. These sonorities lend the movement a new freshness and feeling of vitality.

The coda begins in measure 343 and emphasizes, briefly, hemiola. Throughout, fragments of the main theme are sounded until measure 368, where a C pedal is reached. The pedal heralds the beginning of the movement's solemn close. The "Piú lento" (meas. 371), is marked by a decided slowing of tempo and a pianissimo dynamic level. A grave austerity, interrupted intermittently by pizzicati passages in the strings, brings the movement to a close.

Movement 3

The third movement, "Adagio molto espressivo," is the shortest movement of the First Symphony, but it contains some of the most interesting features of the work. It is cast in a simple three-part form in A-flat major (see Diagram 1–3).

Diagram 1–3. Formal Structure of Third Movement.

		Part 1											
Theme			A			A[1]		(A)					
Key:	A♭:	V	I	V	I^6	I	V	I	V/F	f:i	V$^4_2$	i^6	V/E♭:
MM.:		1	3	6	13	19	25	28	31	32	36	37	39
Comment:		vln.											

									Part 2
Theme:	A			T			(B)		B
Key:	I^6	V	I$^6_4$	I	I	Aug^6	B♭:I	vii$^4_3$/	G:I
MM.:	40	43	46	49	53	56	57	63	64
Comment:									oboe

								Part 3			
Theme:								A			
Key:	B♭:	V^7/V	V	A♭:V/V	V^6	V	V	I	V	V^7	V^7/vi
MM.:	70	71	72	76	79	80	83	84	87	90	95
Comment:	basses							E.H.			

Theme:			A								
Key:	vi	V/vi	vi^6	I	I	V	I	I^6_4	I	V	I
MM.:	96	99	100	102	106	108	109	114	118	123	124
Comment:											

After a two-measure lead-in, the principal theme (A), marked "espressivo," is heard at measure 3 in the first violins (Example 6). It is one of Chadwick's most sweeping melodies, encompassing a wide range (g to d^2), and employing several pungent chromatic tones, most notably the d-natural^1 in measure 4.

The melody is embedded in a thicker texture than is usual in Chadwick's opening statements; here the accompaniment uses the full string section as well as the low woodwinds and horns. Far from being static, the accompaniment figures, often in dialogue with one another, are melodic and graceful. This is one of the most significant aspects of the movement. Throughout movement 3 there is much more independence of individual lines than the listener might expect from hearing Chadwick's earlier music. There is also more juxtaposition of melody upon melody than anywhere else to this point, and less reliance upon simple melody-and-accompaniment figures.

A varied version of the A theme appears in measure 19. Here it is found embellished, with additional tones and greater rhythmic activity. The accompaniment parts, which consist of the same instruments that Chadwick used earlier, are also embellished. The section progresses through F minor (meas. 32), E-flat major (meas. 40), and B-flat major (meas. 57), and finally rests on a diminished chord (meas. 63).

The second part, in G major, opens with an oboe solo, which marks Chadwick's first extended use of that instrument in the symphonies. Throughout this movement, the composer exhibits greater sensitivity to tone color than in the first two movements by his use of an active woodwind section. The woodwinds, along

Example 6. Symphony in C, op. 5, mvt. 3, meas. 2–7.

with the French horn, prove in later works to be among his favorites.

After a brief excursion through B-flat major (meas. 70), the A theme reappears at measure 84, once again in the tonic, A flat. This third part features the theme lushly scored, in unison, for the English horn and clarinet.

Movement 4

The final movement, in sonata form, begins in C major with an introduction marked "Allegro moderato" (see Diagram 1–4).

Diagram 1–4. Formal Structure of Fourth Movement.

	Introduction												
Theme:													
Key:	C:V	V^6	V	V	V	V	V	V	V	V	V—	V	I^6
MM.:	1	6	12	25	31	32	33	40	41	51	52	66	67
Comment:				(S)									

	Part 1 Section 1												
Theme:	P							t					
Key:	IV	I	IV^6	I^6	V	IV	V	I	I^6_4	I	vi	e	Aug^6
MM.:	68	71	76	79	83	88	96	97	102	108	114	116	121
Comment:													

		Part 1 Section 2									
Theme:		S						(P)			
Key:	V/V	C:V	V	V	V/V	V^6	I	V	vi	V	V
MM.:	128	136	144	152	168	170	175	182	194	198	208
Comment:											

Theme:					k						
Key:	e	A	V^7/V	V^6	I	V	V	B	V	c	V
MM.:	210	218	226	233	234	237	244	254	260	268	275
Comment:	chrom. descent				(P)						

	Part 2 Section 3									
Theme:	"Fantasy"									
Key:	c: i	V	i	g	V/E^b	e^b	V/E^b	E^b	F	d
MM.:	276	284	292	300	304	309	315	322	325	331
Comment:	fug. vln I vln II		bsn.	ob.						

Theme:				N	(S)						
Key:	a	d^6	d	d^6	A^b	C	b^b	Aug^6	c	C: I$^6_4$	V^7 I
MM.:	333	341	345	347	355	358	362	367	368	377	381–2
Comment:				dotted rhythms							

				Part 2 Section 4						
Theme:				P						
Key:	V^7	vii$^{o6}_5$/C:	I	IV	I	IV^6	I	A^7	B^b	B V
MM.:	384	387	392	393	396	401	404	409	414	418–21
Comment:		Chad. trans.								

Theme:	t							(S)				
Key:	I	V	I	a	a	c	V	I^6	I	I	vi	I
MM.:	422	432	433	439	441	447	455	461	465	481	488	492
Comment:			(cf. meas. 276)									

Theme:					k			
Key:	IV	I	IV	I$^6_4$	I	V	ii	vi
MM.:	495	496	499	503	507	510	512	514
Comment:								

Theme:								
Key:	ii	I$^6_4$	I	I	A	V/V	V/V	V
MM.:	517	521	523	533	535	543	545	551
Comment:					chrom. descent			

Theme:								Coda I
Key:	V^7	I	IV	IV	Aug^6	V^7/V	vii^{o7}/E	C:I$^6_4$
MM.:	555	562	582	595	603	607	610	611
Comment:								

								Coda II		
Theme:										
Key:	vi	ii	vi	$vii^{\o 4}_{3}$/V	ii	I^{6}_{4}	V	I	a	I^{6}
MM.:	619	627	633	639	645	647	649	651	661	664
Comment:										

Theme:											
Key:	I	V/V	V^{6}	I	E	A^{b}	E^{b}	E	a	Aug^{6}	I^{6}_{4}
MM.:	667	676	680	681	685	687	690	694	695	696	697
Comment:											

				Coda III				
Theme:								
Key:	V	I	V	I	V	I	vi	I
MM.:	701	709	724	725	740	741	744	745
Comment:								

The introduction is by far the longest in the First Symphony, lasting until measure 67. It is divided into two subsections; the first subsection presents an important idea in measure 25, which is later varied slightly to become the theme associated with the secondary tonal area (i.e., S). The introductory character is maintained by the sectional nature of this brief opening. Material is repeated, tempo is frequently manipulated, and there are several fermatas that halt the expression of a complete idea. This subsection lasts until the fermata at measure 51. After the fermata, there follows an extended dominant upbeat (meas. 52 to 66) that leads directly into the exposition.

The theme associated with the principal key (P) is played by the woodwinds and upper strings. Beginning on the subdominant, it is a simple, jolly tune that displays Chadwick's predilection for syncopation (Example 7). The theme lends itself to a great deal of development, particularly as far as rhythm is concerned. Parts of the dancelike melody may easily be dissected and placed in new contexts that allow for further exploitation, and Chadwick made much of the possibilities.

After the transition is reached in measure 97, there is an important imitative idea in measure 116 that leads into the contrasting key area, the dominant, in measure 136. The theme associated with the dominant (S) is the first of many marchlike, thinly scored themes that appear throughout Chadwick's symphonic oeuvre. Here the theme is presented in the lower woodwinds and horns (Example 8).

Example 7. Symphony in C, op. 5, mvt. 4, meas. 68–75.

Example 8. Symphony in C, op. 5, mvt. 4, meas. 136–143.

As mentioned earlier, this theme is related to the theme found in the first subsection of the introduction (cf. meas. 25). The theme as it appears here is well-articulated, and somewhat less martial than before. Chadwick's scoring of this section for woodwinds, rather than brass, accounts for this slight stylistic change. Marked "poco marcato," the melody clearly sounds the new key, although the accompaniment at this point does not demarcate the tonality as well as might be expected. The offbeat rhythm of the accompaniment beginning in measure 135, as well as the use of inverted harmonies, leave the tonality ambiguous. This situation is momentary, and the ambiguity is resolved by the end of the phrase.

The theme associated with the principal key returns at measure 182 in the dominant (G). The remainder of the section from this point on is unusually developmental. The music moves through a variety of tonalities, including E minor (meas. 210), A major (meas. 218), and D major (meas. 226). The changes in tonality are accompanied by thematic material employed in traditionally developmental ways (i.e., fragmentation at meas. 208, augmentation at meas. 220, etc.). The section and the first part end at measure 275 on the dominant.

The development begins in measure 276 in C minor. It is a brief section, lasting just over 100 bars, but it shows a good deal of confidence and competence by the young composer. The section begins with a fugato introduced by the second violins (Example 9). The subject of the fugato was presented earlier, in measure 116, where its appearance was a preparation for its further development in this section. This subject has an ominous, dark character, eventually progressing to outline a C-minor triad. This character is maintained as the theme progresses to the first violins, then to the bassoons and low strings.

The development section is extremely unstable harmonically. The music moves quickly through a variety of keys, beginning in

Example 9. Symphony in C, op. 5, mvt. 4, meas. 276–280.

C minor (meas. 276) and progressing through B-flat major (meas. 304), E-flat minor (meas. 309), F major (meas. 325), D minor (meas. 331), and A-flat major (meas. 355). Throughout this section Chadwick also reintroduced themes and motives, drawing especially upon ideas found in the introduction. At measure 347 a new, dotted-rhythm motive appears, which is quick to proliferate throughout the entire orchestra. There is little stability in the remainder of the section until a "Chadwickian" unison bridge sounds in the strings at measure 387 to lead into the recapitulation.

Section 4 begins at measure 393 on the subdominant, as in the exposition. Chadwick took the opportunity in this section to develop some of his ideas further. At first there is little deviation from what one might expect of a recapitulation. The theme associated with the principal key is sounded in the tonic; the fugal idea from the transition and the development appears in measure 433; the theme associated with the secondary key sounds in the tonic in measure 461. At measure 507 the tempo becomes "poco animato," and the music progresses through a series of harmonies that have rarely been heard previously, including the supertonic (meas. 512) and the submediant (meas. 514). D minor sounds in measure 517, and an extended chromatic descent from A to D begins in measure 535. Several measures emphasizing the subdominant begin at measure 582, before the section comes to its end in measure 611. Clearly, the music of the recapitulation is highly developmental; the first half of this section proceeds in the expected manner, but after reaching the "poco animato" (meas. 507), the music broadens to include greater harmonic variety, thematic manipulation, and other traditionally developmental procedures.

The work ends with a three-section coda, each section of which emphasizes the tonic key, although the second one, beginning at measure 651, journeys into other tonalities including A minor (meas. 661), E major (meas. 685), and A-flat major (meas. 687). The E flat can be understood as the dominant of A flat (meas. 690). Even in the closing section, therefore, the music ventures rather far afield, as if the composer could not resist continuing to breathe life into his creation. It is already evident from this first effort in the genre of the symphony that, in his coda sections, Chadwick enjoyed such effects as changing meters (as between sections 2 and 3 of the present coda), pitting triple rhythm against duple rhythm (meas. 611), and generally forging a bold, rousing ending.

A comparison of the first and the fourth movements of the First Symphony reveals a great deal of structural similarity between the two. While movement 1 begins with a few introductory measures and movement 4 has an extended introduction, the expositions of both are straightforward, presenting their principal themes in the tonic key and moving on to present the theme associated with the secondary key. The sole oddity is the appearance of the secondary theme in E minor in the first movement, thus employing a contrasting mode rather than simply the dominant tonality as the polarity-creating element in the movement. The third section of each movement is, as expected, highly developmental. Perhaps more unusual for a young composer is that every section, with the possible exception of the exposition, is manipulated extensively, including the recapitulation.

Similarly, both movements have multi-sectional codas that introduce new ideas as well as continue the development of old ones. While the themes of each movement are spirited and work very well for sonata form, and the harmonies are often fresh and cleverly employed, the music loses its verve by its sheer length and repetition of ideas. In his First Symphony, it is likely that Chadwick employed nearly every compositional technique that he knew. This would account for the variety, richness, and even the repetitiousness in his first effort.

CRITICAL RECEPTION

The First Symphony is one of Chadwick's least-heralded works, virtually unknown by scholars of American music and totally unknown to modern audiences. The single review that the symphony received was lukewarm, but one may be reasonably certain that the young composer was most happy to receive it. The review appeared in the *Boston Evening Transcript* on February 24, 1882 and focused primarily on Chadwick's use of form and thematic development. The anonymous critic prefaced his comments on the symphony by stating that "to judge of [*sic*] a work of the pretensions and importance of a symphony, by any writer, on a single hearing, is hardly safe."[9] The critic went on to discuss what he thought were the most redeeming characteristics of the composition, as follows:

> Mr. Chadwick's symphony . . . is so clearly formed on such a thoroughly musicianly model, that one may place a reasonable amount of confidence in his first impressions. It was apparent, for instance, that the composer had endeavored to produce a work which should be truly symphonic; one, that is, in which the theme should be regularly developed or treated, as one may say, with genuine symphonic respect. The themes are modest and graceful, and the orchestral treatment is refined and discreet. The color is used with careful judgment, it being the evident intention of the composer to employ it solely for the purpose of bringing his forms into fine relief, and to be neither lavish or niggardly in his resources. Altogether, the young author has reason to be proud of the result of his labors.[10]

As mentioned previously, the critic did not give the impression that he was particularly enthusiastic about the First Symphony. He did, however, sound the major themes that echo throughout the reception history of Chadwick's symphonic output: high-quality craftsmanship, competent handling of developmental procedures, elegant and tuneful melodies, and finely honed orchestration.

CHAPTER 4

SYMPHONY NO. 2 IN B-FLAT MAJOR, OP. 21

HISTORY

Chadwick's Second Symphony was composed between 1883 and 1885 in Boston. The second movement, a scherzo, was the first to be composed and was actually premiered on March 8, 1884, well over a year before the first movement, originally titled "Overture in B-flat" or "Introduction and Allegro," was premiered on April 29, 1885. Victor Yellin suspects that Chadwick, having composed a sonata-form movement and an orchestral scherzo, then decided to add a slow movement and a finale to complete the four-movement structure of a symphony.[1] The symphony, dedicated to a close friend of Chadwick's, A. T. Scott (n.d.), was first performed as a whole by the Boston Symphony Orchestra on December 10, 1886, under the baton of Chadwick himself.[2]

The Second Symphony is cast in the expected four-movement plan, and, as in the First Symphony, the slow movement is in the third position. This work exhibits a wealth of originality that was not present in the earlier symphony. It presents several new harmonic and melodic procedures, as well as innovative techniques in orchestration and a more imaginative use of rhythm. Chadwick also unified the composition with cyclical treatment among the first, third, and fourth movements (significantly, not the second) of the symphony, a technique that was lacking in the First Symphony. In short, this work reflects a significant change in Chadwick's thought about symphonic procedures.

At least some of these changes may be traced to a work composed between the First and Second Symphonies. Before Chadwick completed the second movement of the Second Symphony in 1883, he had composed and published a "concert-overture"

BOSTON:
ARTHUR P. SCHMIDT & Co.,
13 and 15 West Street.

Copyright 1888, Arthur P. Schmidt & Co

Figure 2. Title page, Symphony No. 2 in B♭ Major, op. 21.

entitled *Thalia*. This work is of interest for several reasons. First, it is a continuation of Chadwick's interest in composing works that are light in character. In this composition, named for the muse of comedy, he continued to write in the tuneful vein that he had initiated with the *Rip Van Winkle* Overture and carried through to the First Symphony, while also continuing to develop and manipulate themes skillfully. Second, the *Thalia* Overture exhibits the colorful instrumentation that would become important in the later symphonies. Here the piccolo, first used in the final movement of the First Symphony, appears, as does a battery of percussion instruments, including tambour basque, castanets, and triangle. A critic wrote that for *Thalia* Chadwick

> used a very full orchestra, the richest of scoring, in a work of intrinsically light character, gaining thereby an oriental gorgeousness of color, but without overloading the work, and without recalling the coarse blare of a brass band—a feat by no means too common these days, and the successful performance of which requires a rare knowledge of the orchestra.[3]

ANALYSIS

Movement 1

The first movement of the Second Symphony begins with an extended introduction that takes the music directly into the main section of this sonata-form movement (see Diagram 2–1).

Diagram 2–1. Formal Structure of First Movement.

	Introduction											
Theme:	O^1	O^1	O^2	O^3	O^3			O^3		O^1		
Key:	D		vii^{o7}/B	vi		ii^7	$B^{\flat 6}_{4}$:I			V	D—D	
MM.:	1	5	9	17	22	25		26	31	33	34	38
Comment:												

		Part 1 Section 1				Part 1 Section 2			
Theme:		P	P	T^1		S	K^1	K^2	K^3
Key:	V/B♭:I	I	I	I	V/V	F:I	I	I	I
MM.:	46	50	78	81	103	104	120	142	159
Comment:		(O^1)					$\frac{9}{8}$	$\frac{3}{4}$	

	Part 2 Section 3							Part 2 Section 4		
Theme:	P	T^2						P	T^1	T^2
Key:	(B^b)	Aug^6		G			V/B^b:	I		
MM.:	189	221	248/49	270	286		292	294	310	322
Comment:			hem.		(false recap.)					

Theme:	S	K^1	K^1	n	Coda 1	Coda 2	Coda 3	
Key:	I	I		V	I	I	I	I
MM.:	341	361	379	414	422	454	462	473
Comment:					Assai animato	Presto	¢	

The movement begins curiously in that, while the symphony is in B-flat major, the introduction is clearly in D major. The horn opens the work with a solemn horn call that is the basis of much of the rest of the movement (Example 1).

At measure 5 the chord of D major sounds and the horn call (O^1) is played by the first flute in dialogue with the strings. An eerie, somewhat impressionistic effect is created by the composer's employment of harmonics in the first violins (meas. 5), as well as the pizzicato in the low strings, and the faraway echo of the horn (meas. 5 to 9). A new idea (O^2) is played by the violins in measure 9, where a half-diminished seventh chord built on C sounds. Also important at this point is the appearance of a dotted rhythm in the bassoon and horn parts. After progressing through a series of chromatic harmonies, the music reaches yet another idea (O^3) in measure 17 in the woodwinds (Example 2). It is a languishing, slow-moving theme that is accompanied by dotted rhythms in the horn parts (cf. meas. 9). The repetitiveness of the accompaniment builds steadily in the strings until measure 22, where the first violins enter with the O^3 theme. The music modulates to B-flat

Horn I

Example 1. Symphony No. 2, op. 21, mvt. 1, meas. 1–5.

Example 2. Symphony No. 2, op. 21, mvt. 1, meas. 17–20

major in measure 26, where the O[3] theme appears again, here in both violin parts. The accompaniment role is passed to the woodwinds and horns, where the divided parts lend a rich, thick texture to the whole. Fragments of the opening horn call are played throughout the orchestra. They appear first in the woodwinds (meas. 31) and then are sounded by the horns and strings (meas. 32) The fragments take the music to the final measure of the introduction (meas. 37) where a half-diminished chord built on A leads to the next section.

More introductory material is played at the "Allegro con brio" (meas. 38). The section begins clearly in D major, with flourishes in the first violins outlining the triad. The music begins to modulate in measure 42, and finally progresses to the dominant of B flat in measures 46. This leads to the exposition, in the key of B flat, which is reached in measure 50.

The first theme of the exposition (P), played by the first flute and horns, is closely related to the opening horn call (meas. 1). Far from being presented alone, however, the theme is accompanied here by the entire orchestra, fortissimo. A stark contrast to the first four measures of the theme is sounded in measure 54, where the strings and the first bassoon combine to produce a gentle response to the preceding measures. In measure 58, the music reaches a dominant-seventh chord built on C, where imitation occurs between the woodwinds and the strings. Wagner's influence may be heard here: Not only is the orchestration in the imitative passage by Chadwick similar to a passage in the Prelude to *Die Meistersinger von Nürnberg,* (mm. 101–105) but there is an astonishing similarity of melodic gesture.

Chadwick's use of transitional material (meas. 74) also bears a striking resemblance to a technique employed by Wagner, which relies heavily on scalar string passages (Again, see Prelude to *Die Meistersinger von Nürnberg,* mm. 37–40). It should also be recalled that this type of "Chadwickian" transition occurred in the final movement of the First Symphony (meas. 387). Bearing in mind these similarities, and considering Wagner's fame throughout Europe, it seems obvious that Chadwick was familiar with the works of Wagner.

In measure 78 the music reaches the principal theme but swiftly progresses to another transitional string passage (meas. 81–84). A transitional theme appears in measure 86 and finally leads to the next section, which begins in measure 104.

The secondary area, in the dominant key, F major, is marked by a horn solo (meas. 105). The woodwinds take up the theme in measure 113, and eventually the music progresses to a closing passage (meas. 120) where the strings are featured in scalar passages (meas. 142). Dialogue occurs between the upper and lower strings, while the winds take on a static accompaniment role. The scalar material continues, although somewhat altered, in measure 142. A third closing area is reached in measure 159 and features hemiola (meas. 159 to 166) throughout the fabric of the orchestra. Reminiscences of the opening horn motive occur in the woodwinds (meas. 177) and take the music into the next section.

The development section, among the shortest in Chadwick's symphonic oeuvre at just over 100 measures, begins with the opening motive played by the horns in B flat (meas. 189). The dominant of E flat is reached in measure 193, where the opening motive begins to appear throughout the orchestra. As the section develops momentum, an E-flat pedal is reached (meas. 201), as is a new theme, derived from the opening.

The E-flat pedal is resolved in measure 213, beginning with a progression of half-diminished and augmented-sixth chords. The chords are not resolved in a predictable manner; they are used for their coloristic effect, not their functionality. It is often difficult to determine the tonality of the music. Although harmonic instability is a feature of development sections, such total lack of tonal centers for a long period of time is not necessarily consistent with developmental procedure. Most often, music undergoing development passes through various keys; avoidance of any sense of tonal center is not the usual goal.

The progression begins in measure 213, where a half-diminished chord sounds. This sonority is followed by a half-diminished chord built on F (meas. 215), an augmented-sixth chord (meas. 217), a half-diminished chord built on C (meas. 218), a half-diminished chord built on D, and an augmented-sixth chord (meas. 221). This progression is followed by a transitional area that takes the music, via a chromatic descent from A flat, to the dominant in measure 226. Development continues in measure 228, where another half-diminished chord sounds, leading the music to a C-major chord in measure 230. This begins a rapid progression through a variety of keys (Table 1).

Key:	C	f	E	D	e	D	G	B^{b}
Measure:	230	234	241	245	253	260	270	286

Table 1. Symphony No. 2, op. 21, mvt. 1, meas. 230–286.

The thematic material in the development is varied; the horn call used in the introduction sounds throughout the orchestra (meas. 245–51), and much is made of scalar passages (meas. 234, 238, 253, 254, and elsewhere). Rhythmic displacement occurs in the development (meas. 243–251), and hemiola figures prominently (meas. 249–251, 263–266).

The recapitulation is heralded by the move to B-flat major (meas. 286), where the horn call is played and accompaniment figures similar to those of the exposition sound. It is not the beginning of a new section, but rather the end of the development; a Chadwickian transitional phrase is reached in measure 292, which leads the music into the next section. This section is straightforward and varies little from the exposition, except that the strings are included in the playing of the horn-call figure, and the brass takes a more active accompanimental role. Otherwise, themes and harmonies progress in an expected manner. The theme associated with the secondary key is presented in the tonic (meas. 341), this time by the trumpet (cf. meas. 104). The static nature of the accompaniment at this point gives an impression of uneasy calmness before the music progresses through one of Chadwick's characteristic transitions (meas. 357) to the next area.

The closing section of the recapitulation is reached in measure 361. At this point, the manipulation of scales is once again highlighted (cf. meas. 124). Triple rhythms are exploited while the music progresses through a variety of tonalities. The general movement of the section does not differ significantly from that of the exposition. Sixteenth-note scalar passages begin in measure 379 (cf. meas. 142), and the music progresses to B-flat major in measure 396. Shortly thereafter (meas. 398), a large section of hemiola is sounded. The dominant arrives in measure 404, and a dominant pedal is reached in measure 414 where the style of the music suddenly changes. Marked "più mosso," held notes occur in the winds while the upper strings play eighth notes. The music proceeds to the tonic in measure 422, where the first part of a three-part coda begins.

The first part of the coda employs material based on the principal theme in the horns and woodwinds, while the strings continue the eighth-note passage from the previous section. Another large hemiola section is reached in measure 430.The tonal movement reaches B major in measure 438. The dominant is reached in measure 453, and takes the music to the next section of the coda. The second part of the coda is a brief transitional section, marked "Presto," that leads into part 3 in measure 462. The final part hints at the opening horn call theme before reaching the fortissimo ending in measure 473.

Movement 2

The second movement, a sonata-form "Allegretto scherzando" in F major, is one of the best-known works in the repertoire of the "Boston Classicists" (see Diagram 2–2).

Diagram 2–2. Formal Structure of Second Movement.

		Part 1 Section 1					Part 1 Section 2			
Theme:		P			P	t^1	S		(P)	
Key:	F:	I	(A)	V	I	V	C:I	V		I—I
MM.:	1	5	11	21	35	39	45	53	54	68 76
Comment:							(B)	g pedal		

		Part 2 Section 3								
Theme:			P			t^2	L			
Key:	vii^{o7}/F:	V^4_3	I	(A)	V	I	iii	V———		V
MM.:	77–80	81	85	94	104	105	121	127	138	156
Comment:							(legato P)			

	Part 2 Section 4									Coda
Theme:	P			S		(P)		t		N/P
Key:	I	(A)	V	I	V^7		I^6_4	I—	—I	
MM.:	157	164	172	185	193	195	197	208	216	217
Comment:			(cf. meas. 21)							

Theme:	(P)	(P)			
Key:		I^6_4	V^7	I——	—I
MM.:	225	229	232	233	251
Comment:					

After four introductory measures, the first theme is introduced at the upbeat to measure 5 by a solo oboe (Example 3).

The solo sounds nearly pentatonic, built on the pitches FCGDA, a "tonal" pentatonic scale.[4] Additions to the scale, which prevent it from being perfectly pentatonic, consist of several appearances of the pitch-class E, including the final note of the phrase, an e^2 that functions as dominant of the key of A major, to which the passage modulates. This movement is frequently noted for its use of pentatonicism, and its introduction of a tone outside of the pentatonic scale is not unusual. In an article on pentatonicism in Dvořák's String Quartet in F, op. 96 ("The American"), David Beveridge writes that

> most often in Western art and folk music the pentatonic scale is not treated as a closed system to be followed strictly for any great length of time. In fact, what we think of as the pentatonic feeling may be more dependent on certain peculiarities of melodic motion than on strict adherence to the scale.[5]

It is Chadwick's application of "certain peculiarities of melodic motion" that give this melody its pentatonic "feel." Most frequently, the pitches not included in the pentatonic scale are sim-

Example 3. Symphony No. 2, op. 21, mvt. 2, meas. 5–8.

ple passing tones that go by so quickly as hardly to be noticed (i.e., the pitch class E in meas. 5 and 9). The e^1 in measure 7 is clearly employed to emphasize the pungency of the half-diminished seventh chord that precedes measure 8 and to heighten the effect of the phrase ending; Beveridge would call the use of tones outside the pentatonic cell to lend a pentatonic effect the "fresh note principle."[6] In fact, the nearness of the e^1 to g^1 helps to make it sound as though it is a member of the pentatonic scale because in the pentatonic context the minor third is a normally occurring interval; therefore the e^1 does not disturb the general impression of pentatonicism. After a transition at measure 39, the secondary area is reached in measure 45.

The secondary area begins in the key of C major, but prominent B flats are found throughout the section. In fact, to say that the area is in C gives a mistaken impression of Chadwick's style of harmonic development. Throughout, the music lapses into odd, sometimes very distant keys, including a journey through E major in measures 51 and 52, and an unusual progression from measure 61 to 68 (Table 2).

Harmony:	C:	$\text{vii}^{0}{}^{6}_{5}/\text{IV}$	$\flat\text{VI}^{6}_{4}$	$\text{vii}^{0}{}^{4}_{3}$	VII	$\text{vii}^{o}{}^{4}_{2}/\text{V}$
Measure:		61	62	63	64	65

Harmony:	III	vi-V	I
Measure:	66	67	68

Table 2. Symphony No. 2, op. 21, mvt. 2, meas. 61–68

The new theme in this section is one of Chadwick's most charming and playful melodies, owing to the gentle descent of the oboes and clarinets, complete with grace notes. There follows an ascending figure in the horns, bassoons, and strings (meas. 45).

It is not long until hints of the main theme return (meas. 54). The development is reached in measure 81, where the music begins a dialogue among several instruments based on the theme associated with the principal key. A complete statement of the main theme is heard in the oboe part beginning in measure 85. The theme is spread to several instruments before it begins to break up near measure 97. At this point the music begins to exploit various rhythmic cells until, at measure 121, a variation of the main theme is reached in augmentation. A transition begins in measure 143 with an E pedal in the bass. Above the pedal is a dialogue among the instruments, similar to that found in measure 81.

The recapitulation begins in measure 157, where the opening theme is clearly sounded, but in a new register, and this time by the violins. The contrasting theme appears in the tonic in measure 185, and, after a transition in measure 208, the coda is reached in measure 217. At this point a new theme (N), striking in its orchestration, is played by the oboe and first horn. Marked "cantabile," this lyrical melody is notable for its nearly pentatonic structure, which gives it a somewhat Dvořákian character. With the exception of the e^2 in measure 221, it is entirely pentatonic. The new theme is surrounded by fragments of the opening theme heard throughout the string section.

Movement 3

Movement 3, marked "Largo e maestoso," begins in D minor. It is in a somewhat unusual five-part (ABCDA) form, one that Chadwick had not constructed in his symphonic movements until now (see Diagram 2–3).

Diagram 2–3. Formal Structure of Third Movement.

		Part 1										
Theme:		A				t^1		B				(A)
Key:	d:	i	i	V/a:i	i	III	V	i	d:V/V	V—	V	i
MM.:	1	5	8	11	12	13	20	21	28	29	32	33
Comment:								A pedal				

Theme:			k							
Key:	i	V	i	iv^6_4	iv^6_4	VI	iv	iv^6	i	V/G
MM.:	36	39	40	42	44	50	52	54	57	62
Comment:			D pedal							

	Part 2					Part 3					
Theme:	C					D			(D)		
Key:	g:i	i	iv	iv	V/B^b:	I	V	V/C:	I	I	Aug^6
MM.:	63	67	71	75	87	88	96	103	104	111	119
Comment:											

	Part 4		Part 5					
Theme:	t^2		A			B	A	B
Key:	V/d——	—V/d:	i	i	V——	—V	i—i	vii^{o7}/iv
MM.:	120	156	157	161	164	172	184	192
Comment:						A pedal		

Theme:									
Key:	iv	V	D:I——	—I	vii^{o6}_{5}	I	iv	I	I
MM.:	193	198	199	203	207	208	213	214	216
Comment:	d pedal					hem.			

After four introductory measures that recall the opening measures of the first movement of this symphony, the morose, slow-moving main theme, which emphasizes the D minor triad, begins in measure 5. It is sounded in the violins and violas, while the lower strings and timpani accompany the tune. The theme cadences on A minor in measure 12 and moves back into D minor at measure 28, where once again the main theme is heard, this time in the woodwinds. The theme is accompanied by scalar passages in the string section, as well as fanfare gestures in the trumpet part and rolls in the timpani. At tonic pedal from measure 40 to 52 takes the section to its close, with two measures of hemiola (meas. 59 and 60) providing an effective cadential ritardando.

At measure 63, the music arrives at Part 2 in the minor subdominant, G minor. This section acts as a brief transition to Part 3. It is characterized by woodwind tremolos, fanfarelike brass figures, and rapid movement in the strings. The sudden changes in dynamic levels, as well as the general character of the music at this point, suggest the comparison of this section to the beginning of Saint-Saëns's Symphony No. 3 (1886). While Chadwick was certainly influenced by the French master throughout his career, he arrived at this particular passage independently from Saint-Saëns's work, for Chadwick's symphony was composed first.

Part 3 begins in measure 88, where a new theme (D) appears in B flat. The theme, heard in the viola part, is very festive (Example 4). The jubilant quality of this theme is due not only to its major modality, but also to its rousing, fast-paced accompaniment in $\frac{6}{8}$ meter. The accompaniment begins with fanfare figures in the trumpets in measure 88, which are followed by similar figures in

Example 4. Symphony No. 2, op. 21, mvt. 3, meas. 88–94.

the woodwinds. These figures are heard again in the upper woodwinds and violins in measure 96 in F major, and are accompanied by the horn-fifth figure, played by the horns. At measure 104, the theme is heard in the lower brass and lower string parts in C major. Again the horn-fifth figure is heard, here played by the oboes. The section ends with an augmented-sixth chord in measure 119 that leads directly into Part 4.

Part 4, marked "Allegro con fuoco," presents new material that acts primarily as a prolonged upbeat to the final section. This section is characterized by a great deal of rhythmic vigor; dialogue occurs between the brass and woodwind instruments (meas. 128 to 133), and the strings are extremely active throughout. A dominant harmony appears in measure 156 and leads into Part 5.

The final section appears in measure 157, where the primary theme returns in the tonic. The music employs the full orchestra at this point, with the theme heard in the woodwinds. The brass instruments accompany with fanfare figures, while the strings perform rapid, descending scalar passages. In measure 173, the strings play the B theme (cf. meas. 21) until the reappearance of the A theme in measure 184 in D minor. By measure 199 the music has reached D major (although a hint of D minor appears in measure 208). Chadwick's interest in hemiola as a way of producing a cadential ritardando is once again apparent in measures 208–213. The movement closes in measure 216 in D major.

Movement 4

The fourth movement of the Second Symphony, "Allegro molto animato," is another example of Chadwick's typical rousing, finalelike ending (cf. Symphony in C major, op. 5, mvt. 1, meas. 537). The movement, in B flat, begins without an introduction, the first sonata-form movement among Chadwick's symphonies to do so (see Diagram 2–4).

Diagram 2–4. Formal Structure of Fourth Movement.

Part 1
Section 1

Theme:	P^1			P^2			
Key:	B^b:I	V	V^7	I	I	vii^{o7}/V	V^6_4
MM.:	1	8	22	23	27	29	31
Comment:				(cf. mvt. 3, meas. 88)			

Theme:			t^1			
Key:	V/V	V/A^b		V/V	V	V^7/V
MM.:	32	34	36	39	40	48
Comment:						

Part 1
Section 2

Theme:	S	(S)			t^2				P^1		
Key:	F:I	V/IV	IV—	IV	I^6—	I^6	I	V	I	V^7	vi
MM.:	50	57	58	68	70	74	75	81	82	83	84
Comment:											

Part 2
Section 3

Theme:									(P^1)	
Key:	V^7	I	V	D^b:I	vi^6_4	IV	ii	Aug^6	F:V^6_4	I
MM.:	87	88	95	96	100	104	106	108	112	116
Comment:				(cf. mvt. 3, meas. 5)						

Theme:	P^1+S				P^1					
Key:	f——	f	b^b	g	D^b		Aug^6	B^b:I^6_4		E^b:V
MM.:	123	127	131	133	135	136	141	143	146	150
Comment:						linear descent			(cf. mvt. 3, meas. 5)	

Part 2
Section 4

Theme:	P^1			P^1		S				
Key:	I			B^b:I	V	I	V^7	IV	V^4_2	V
MM.:	151	155	156	158	165	178	181	186	194	197
Comment:	IV/B^b		(cf. mvt. 1, meas. 1)							

Theme:	t^2		(P^1)			S			k	
Key:	I^6	I^6	V	I	I	III	III	+II		V^6/V
MM.:	198	202	214	219	223	227	235	237	239	248
Comment:				trpts.			ob.		(cf. mvt. 4, meas. 36)	

Theme:	P^1			(S)		Coda P^2			
Key:	V^7	I	I_4^6	V^7/V	V	I	V_4^6	I——	I
MM.:	251	254	256	262	264	266	288	308	332
Comment:									

The first tonic-key theme is a vibrant, rhythmic melody played by the upper woodwinds and strings (Example 5). Measures 3 and 4 are derived from the introduction of the first movement, just one instance of cyclic treatment in the symphony.

A second theme in the tonic (P^2) occurs in measure 23. It is a slight variation of a theme from Part 3 of the third movement (cf. meas. 88). This marks the first time that Chadwick introduced a clearly defined second theme in the tonic area of the exposition of his symphonies. Here Chadwick borrowed the entire fabric from his third movement, casting the melody in the bassoons and cellos, while the accompanying horn-fifth figures are played by the upper strings.

In the exposition of this movement Chadwick introduced several new and important techniques into his compositional style. It includes the composer's first attempts to create unity among the movements of a work by employing in one movement melodic material from another movement. Chadwick's introduction of a second theme in the tonic key is another innovation that will prove to be important in later works.

After a brief transition in measure 36, the secondary area occurs

Example 5. Symphony No. 2, op. 21, mvt. 4, meas. 1–4.

in measure 50. The theme of the dominant-key area (Example 6a) immediately reminds one of passages from Dvořák's Symphony No. 9 in E minor, op. 95 ("From the New World") (Example 6b). The passages share the same general melodic contour, as well as traits of orchestration and rhythm, but, while Chadwick's music may seem to echo Dvořák, in this instance the reverse is the case; Dvořák's famous symphony was not composed until 1893, nearly a decade after Chadwick's symphony. It is not known whether Dvořák had the opportunity to familiarize himself with Chadwick's work before his Ninth Symphony was composed.

In measure 52, the music begins a passage of stark chromaticism that seems oddly out of place both harmonically and melodically. As the music twists briefly by half steps and minor thirds, before again sounding the theme in the upper strings (meas. 54), it is as if Chadwick intended to alarm the listener by the jarring use of chromaticism, just after a diatonic/pentatonic passage. The remainder of the section includes an astonishing amount of

Example 6a. Symphony No. 2, op. 21, mvt. 4, meas. 50–54.

Example 6b. Dvořák, Symphony No. 9 in E minor, op. 95 ("From the New World"), mvt. 1, meas. 53–56.

thematic development; as early as measure 60, the music is altered and manipulated. Fragments of the first theme in this movement (P^1) are sounded in measure 82 in F major. This signals a transition to the next section.

The development begins in measure 96 with an abrupt shift into the key of D flat. This modulation starts one of Chadwick's most compact and complex development sections. The theme of this section is, once again, borrowed from movement 3 of this symphony (cf. mvt. 3, meas. 5). In measure 112 the first theme appears in the key of F major, and there is a change to the minor mode in measure 123. At this point there appears a variety of themes borrowed from earlier movements, as well as those from this movement. The lower strings sound the secondary theme of this movement (cf. meas. 50), while the upper strings sound fragments of the opening of this movement (cf. meas. 1). The woodwinds play augmented figures that are related to the main theme of movement 2 in measures 124–25 (cf. mvt. 2, meas. 5). After passing through B-flat minor (meas. 131), G minor (meas. 133), and D-flat major (meas. 135), the music returns to B-flat major in (meas. 143). Shortly thereafter, in measures 150–51, a fragment of the principal theme (P^1) is played in augmentation in the key of E flat, or IV of the tonic B flat. In measures 151–156, the material from the introduction to the first movement is presented in dialogue fashion between the clarinets, horns, and bassoons.

The recapitulation begins in measure 158 with the main theme. The material associated with the secondary key returns in the tonic in measure 178 in the lower strings, with accompaniment figures found in the upper woodwinds. A solo trumpet plays a fragment of this theme in measure 182, just before it sounds in the trombones in measure 186.

Transitional material occurs in measure 198 and lasts until measure 227, where the cellos play music associated with the secondary key (S), now in the key of D major, looking back to the D-major introduction in the first movement. The theme sounds throughout the orchestra until measure 239, where dotted figures are sounded (cf. meas. 36). This leads to measure 251, where the first principal-key theme is stated once again in the upper strings, closely followed in measure 262 by the final statement of the secondary theme.

The coda begins in measure 266, where the strings play the theme from Part 3 of the third movement (cf. also mvt. 4, meas.

23), in B-flat major. It is accompanied by the horn-fifth figures, played here by the trumpets and horns. After the "Presto" marking in measure 308, where figures again recalling the introduction of the first movement sound in the horns, the Second Symphony closes resolutely in the key of B-flat major in measure 332.

CRITICAL RECEPTION

As mentioned previously, Chadwick's Second Symphony was probably not originally conceived as a multi-movement work. Rather, the composer had composed two individual works, a scherzo and an overture, and decided to employ them as movements of a symphony for which he needed to complete two more movements. Before the work was presented as a whole, the composer allowed at least one performance of the scherzo by itself. The movement was presented by the Boston Symphony Orchestra on March 10, 1884. The critic wrote a glowing review of the movement, stating,

> Mr. Chadwick's new Scherzo is a gem. The themes on which it is built up are both original and taking—the first theme, with its quasi-Irish humorousness (it positively winks at you), is peculiarly happy. The working up of the movement sounds clear and coherent, even at first hearing; the piquant charm of the whole is irresistible. The orchestration is that of a master, and is full of delicious bits of color, without ever becoming outrageous. The impression the Scherzo made was instantaneous, and as favorable as the composer himself could have wished.[7]

Although the anonymous music critic had heard only the scherzo movement of what would soon be the Second Symphony, he touched upon issues that would dominate the writings about this composition in the future. These issues would include Chadwick's originality, "humorousness," coherency, and masterful orchestration. Some of these traits had been foreshadowed in the First Symphony and the *Rip van Winkle* Overture, especially as concerns orchestration in the latter, but the scherzo movement of the Second Symphony has the honor of being Chadwick's first major orchestral success.

The complete work was not without very vocal detractors, however. Upon the first performance of the entire Second Symphony, another anonymous reviewer (possibly the same writer) was less enthusiastic. He wrote,

> Mr. Chadwick's new symphony is a work so unexpected in character that one hardly knows how to take it nor what to say of it. Mr. Chadwick has already shown that he has genuine talent of no common order, and this symphony gives proof of it quite as good as any of his previous works. He has decided melodic invention, and is a good harmonist; he has, too, that which further work and study may develop into a very considerable technique in composition. More than all he has real charm and brilliance; what he writes is alive and sounds spontaneous. In this last Symphony of his there is much that is fascinating—the Scherzo, with which the public is already familiar, is a gem in its way, and the slow movement shows decided originality. And yet there is that in the general character and animus of the symphony which baffles all attempts at comparing it with known models of any school. We, for one, cannot remember any music of this character being written in the symphonic form. One feels like saying, with Friar Lawrence, "Art thou a symphony? Thy form cries out, thou art."[8]

The writer then went on to specify his complaints:

> The general lack of true seriousness in the music; the light, almost operatic, character of the thematic material; the constant changes of rhythm; the frequent solo passages—not merely incidental phrases for this or that instrument, but often full-fledged solos of considerable length—all contribute to make the work fall short of what may be called symphonic dignity. Of the stoutness of the construction and the quality of the workmanship one cannot judge after a single hearing. The work is brilliant, often very fascinating, but it stands fitful, capricious, and, if we may be pardoned for saying so, even frivolous. In the matter of orchestration Mr. Chadwick here falls somewhat short of the standard of some of his previous work, of the Thalia overture, for instance.[9]

Finally, the author penned a few words of encouragement before taking Chadwick to task. He stated, "As we have said, the composition shows genuine talent," and he continues, "But it seems as if the composer had not yet sufficiently drilled his powers to cope with so severe a task as a symphony."[10] One can only imagine the composer's despair after reading these words. The auspicious premiere of the scherzo certainly must have given him hope for the rest of the work, but time after time he garnered reviews that were lukewarm at best.

The music critic of the *Boston Post* reviewed the same concert and was only slightly more encouraging. He began his review,

> Mr. Chadwick has always something interesting to say, even if it is not very deep, and the symphony played Saturday evening is the most interesting of his works that we have yet heard; there are many themes that are both original and striking, and much that is good in the work; . . .[11]

After these kind words, however, the critic quickly pointed out the various flaws as he perceived them:

> . . . the themes are better than their treatment, and there is constant striving for effect at the expense of the true and beautiful. To be more particular, the symphony, to a certain extent, usurps its title; it is more a suite than a symphony. In proof of this it must be said that the first movement has neither the breadth nor the dignity that are demanded of such a piece of music. In one place it actually lapses into a waltz, which is pleasing enough in itself, but is out of place in a symphony. Such things help perhaps to make a work popular with the indiscriminate, but they are to be unreservedly condemned from a just point of view.[12]

The reviewer's comment that the work resembles a suite more than a symphony is one of the most important critical remarks in all of the Chadwick literature, as will be seen in the discussion of the quasi-symphonies. Yet, in his criticism that the symphony does not meet certain standards of "breadth and dignity" required in such a composition, the reviewer's analytical understanding of the work does not appear to have been very secure. For example, he erroneously continues,

> The first and last movements are lacking both in a firm establishment of the tonality and in true organic development.

> These faults give a fragmentary aspect to the whole production, which is out of keeping with the true symphony. The allegro scherzando, placed for no good reason as the second movement, has already been heard here, and is undoubtedly the best that the symphony contains; it is quite original, with a pleasing Scotch flavor, and had a great success with the audience.[13]

Of course, cursory analysis clarifies the tonalities of both movements (although the tonality of D major is somewhat unusual in the introductory section of the first movement), and, while neither movement should be considered a model of organic development, they are certainly not "fragmentary." As for so many other critics, the scherzo was the most favored movement of the work. Of the rest of the symphony, the critic wrote,

> We wish that we had not to criticise the work as a symphony, because from any other standpoint it would be possible to say better things about it; but the composer challenges attention to the work as a symphony, and as such we are bound to consider it. The third movement departs from the usual custom, and with no good effect, by having an interpolated allegro. It has worthy moments, but, as we said before, the treatment is not as good as the idea. In the last movement some clever use is made of themes taken from the previous movements, but the constant changes of tonality and tempo give this movement a certain patchwork character which is much to be regretted.[14]

Finally, the critic ended by scolding,

> Mr. Chadwick, who is capable of better things, has sacrificed artistic truth to a desire to please and to produce brilliant effects; and he will come to grief if he persists in writing symphonies, at any rate, in this vein. The applause and enthusiasm were, for a Boston audience, almost unbounded at the conclusion of the symphony, and the composer was enthusiastically recalled.[15]

In yet another review, this time by the *Boston Herald,* the reviewer gave an extremely positive assessment of the symphony. Beginning with a reminiscence of the First Symphony, the *Herald* reviewer wrote,

> Mr. Chadwick's first effort in symphony writing was heard during the past season of public concerts given by the Harvard Musical Association, some five years ago, and the ability shown by this composer in his first symphony made the work of last evening one of great interest to the local public.[16]

He continued,

> Mr. Chadwick has certainly made a great advance in his second symphony, and the work is a credit to this conscientious musician and composer. No more satisfactory effort in this line of writing has as yet been put before the public by a native born citizen, and its presentation at this time is calculated to give encouragement to the few friends of the American composer.[17]

While the review was not without some negative criticism, the reviewer was generally enthusiastic:

> There are some evidences of the youth and inexperience of the composer in the incomplete and fragmentary treatment of the themes in the allegro con brio movement, and in the somewhat labored construction of the opening portion of the final movement; but, aside from these comparative defects, the work is in good form, original and melodious in its themes and skillfully orchestrated. The scherzanda [*sic*] was heard here in these concerts two seasons ago, and the opening movements have had a semi-public performance before now, but as the work was not completed until a year ago it fitly represents the present ability of Mr. Chadwick as a symphonic composer. The scherzanda [*sic*] and largo movements, the latter a peculiarly graceful idea, are the most enjoyable portion of the work, each showing a fresh, vigorous thought well worked out. The finale of the symphony displays the skill of Mr. Chadwick in orchestral combinations at its best, and leaves a very pleasant idea of the entire composition.[18]

At this early stage in his career, Chadwick was already gaining notoriety for his keen sense of orchestration, an astounding ability that was an asset to him throughout his life.

As mentioned in Chapter 1, Chadwick long harbored the desire of conducting professionally. While he had conducted the premiere of his First Symphony with the Harvard Musical Association, this was his first attempt at conducting one of his symphonies before a fully professional ensemble. The writer of the present review seems not to have taken great notice of Chadwick's abilities on the podium, briefly stating:

> The symphony was directed by the composer with good success, save in portions of the last movement, in which there was a lack of clearness in the presentation of the somewhat intricate development of this portion of the work.[19]

Another anonymous music critic discussed the premiere performance of the Second Symphony in splendid detail:

> What is plainly avoided by the composer is the realistic method; Mr. Chadwick is no improver of Wagner. He writes after the precepts of Mendelssohn and with something of Gade's vigor and sense of color. His good technical training is shown in the general smoothness of contour which all the movements present, and this is the more appreciable, as after a technical examination the more important are found to be fraught with changes of key, rhythm and design. In his instrumentation the composer works with freedom and taste; but there is a tendency to carry the winds out of balance and to seek original effects in a sort of nonchalant manner not compatible with absolute conservatism, and this trend of the composer is apparent in his giving to both the larger movements more a rhapsodical than symphonic character. While such things are expressive of individuality and are often executed with much skill, they are of the nature of an experiment and less in place, and because of this more detrimental, when one has a symphony in hand.[20]

Here again a reviewer gave the impression that he did not find the work sufficiently "dignified" in the traditional symphonic sense. The rhapsodical character of certain movements of the symphony is important as one looks toward later development in the composer's symphonic style, but at any rate, such developments were not exactly revolutionary in the history of the genre. Apparently, the writer was exposing his own biases toward classicism in symphonic composition.

The reviewer continued with his thoughts about Chadwick's orchestration:

> The work abounds in happy fancies, nice effects of combination and harmonious tone-blending; the second subject of the scherzo revives some Beethoven-like twists with the bassoon, while the movement as a whole is both piquant and original. Mr. Chadwick's use of forces in his climaxes makes them stirring and effective, yet there is need of a better plan of action which shall make them the outcome of something imperative, made necessary by what has preceded. There is much beauty in the largo, and if one finds restlessness and motion where quiet would have been preferred, the result is an evidence of the composer's affection for the brasses, without which he could scarcely be called American.[21]

Finally the writer closed with a few remarks about Chadwick's performance as a conductor:

> The composer conducted his own work, and doubtless its performance was less illustrious than it would have been otherwise; it is a proud moment for a composer to take the baton of the symphony orchestra; but the act elevates the individual more than it benefits the work.[22]

As the number of reviews begins to mount, we see the disturbing picture of a conductor getting in the way of the performance of his works rather than enhancing them through proper interpretation and skillful baton work.

The famous critic Philip Hale had only a few words to say about Chadwick and the Second Symphony. He wrote:

> It is a work of long-breath, well-conceived, well-expressed. It is the work of a musician by birth and breed. It is an honor not only to himself but to his country. It shows a strangely-marked, well-defined individuality.[23]

As mentioned earlier, critics were more often taken with the second movement than the other parts of the composition, and likewise it seems to have captured Hale's imagination:

> . . . it's a jolly, jocose movement which approaches the edge of vulgarity . . . . The opening measures might serve to beat out the time to the heavy feet of Roustabouts dancing on the levy [*sic*]. There is a smell of American soil in this same scherza [*sic*]: a suggestion of the good-natured recklessness of the citizens of these states.[24]

Hale concluded,

> Mr. Chadwick's scherzo could only have been written by an American, for its fun is intensely local, as is its color.[25]

The work did not fare well in Chicago, where it was performed at the World's Columbian Exhibition on May 23, 1893 by the Theodore Thomas Orchestra under the direction of assistant conductor Arthur Mees (1850–1923). The performance was harshly reviewed by W.S.B. Mathews (1837–1912), who wrote,

> Mr. Chadwick's symphony upon the present occasion did not quite bear out the composer's reputation of a man who has something to say. Or more properly, while he evidently had something to say, it by no means appeared that the something to say needed such a great deal of noise for saying it. Even the question of time required for the saying was left in some doubt. Many things in the symphony were creditable—perhaps almost all. There were clever bits of writing, and there was an earnestness and manly mood throughout; but after all there was more hard work than the music seemed to warrant. Whether this impression is to be taken as the critic's inability to understand tone-poetry before it has been explained, or whether it is due to the insufficient rehearsal, inadequate interpretation, or whether again it was really well founded are all available suppositions which the reader may treat optionally.[26]

Although Mathews was in fact writing for a music periodical and was a knowledgeable, mostly self-taught musician in his own right, there are a number of problems with his review. Even though he wrote several books about music and was a frequent contributor to *Dwight's Journal of Music,* some of his use of musical jargon is flawed.[27] This is particularly true when he admits his inability to understand "tone-poetry," a term that should have had no part in his discussion to begin with. His incorrect application of terminology at a time when many music critics were very fluent in technical jargon (and, in many cases, overemployed such language) only underscores a basic lack of musical understanding. Fortunately for the composer, most of his criticism fell upon the performance and not the work itself, which, for all its faults, was at least "creditable."

Another review of the Chicago performance does not discuss the music so much as it discusses conditions surrounding the performance. Under the headline "American Music Failed to Draw—After the Clamor For It Only A Hundred Heard the Thomas Orchestra Play It," the reviewer sarcastically stated,

> Patriotism was conspicuously absent at the concert of American compositions given in Music hall [*sic*] yesterday afternoon. Those who had been clamoring for a representation of native talent were well aware of the fact that such a program had been arranged, and yet the audience only numbered 100.[28]

After taking into account other works on the program, the reviewer gave the Second Symphony only brief mention, stating that the work was

> entitled to more careful and analytic consideration than is possible after hearing [it] at a performance in which everything was hopelessly blurred by the wretched acoustics of the hall. That the works are scholarly none will deny. But one of the dangers of scholasticism is the mere exhibition of intensive knowledge without the ability of utilizing it for the creation of new thoughts or of presenting the old ones in new garb.[29]

Chadwick's reaction to this review is not known; perhaps the vagueness of the author's complaints would have caused the Yankee composer to shrug off such unsubstantiated remarks. But we can guess that the critic's final line made more than a few composers angry: "From a musical point of view America has as yet had no message to deliver to the world."[30]

CHAPTER 5

SYMPHONY IN F (NO. 3)

HISTORY

Chadwick's Symphony in F (No. 3) was begun in 1893 and first performed in the following year by the Boston Symphony Orchestra, conducted by the composer. The composition was dedicated to Chadwick's friend and colleague Theodore Thomas.

Chadwick had entered the symphony in the second annual composition competition sponsored by the National Conservatory of Music in New York in 1894.[1] The director of the conservatory at that time was Antonin Dvořák, who had won a great deal of fame in the United States for his promotion of American nationalism and the use of Indian and Negro tunes in symphonic music. The announcement by Dvořák that Chadwick's Third Symphony had taken first prize in the competition came in the *American Art Journal* on April 21, 1894. Under the headline "Chadwick's Symphony Wins the Prize," the announcement read as follows:

> I take pleasure in announcing to you that your Symphony offered for the second annual competition of the National Conservatory of Music has obtained the prize. In view of your desire to produce it without delay, we have decided to waive our right.[2]

The composition differs from the preceding two symphonies in several ways. First, there is much more rhythmic ingenuity and variety here than in either of the preceding symphonies; in fact, some of the composer's attempts to make a section rhythmically interesting resulted in some awkwardness. Second, Chadwick made more effective use of the orchestral palette, especially as far as the brass instruments are concerned. He was more willing than before to employ the brass in choirs, as well as to use them as solo instruments. Third, there are several instances of pentatonicism, some of them quite striking. Inexplicably, the Third Symphony has been almost completely overlooked in Chadwick studies as regards pentatonicism.

Some of the themes of the Third Symphony are far more folklike in character than those Chadwick had used previously. By the early 1890s Chadwick must have been fully aware of the trend toward nationalism in parts of Europe. The use of folklike themes is not new in Chadwick's symphonies, as we have already seen in the Second Symphony and indeed, to a lesser degree, in the First Symphony. There is nothing specifically "American," however, about the themes that he composed; that is, he did not employ well-known folk songs in the works. Rather, he used melodies that are of a pastoral nature and reflect a sincere simplicity that is commonly associated with folk music.

At first the Third Symphony would seem to bear comparison to Brahms's Third Symphony. Chadwick had ample opportunity to become familiar with Brahms's score; the Boston Symphony Orchestra frequently performed the older master's Third Symphony, beginning in 1884. Subsequent performances in 1886, 1888, 1889, and 1892 also featured the composition.[3] The two have several similarities on the surface: Both are in F major, both begin with several measures of ominous chords, and their instrumentation is nearly identical. Furthermore, throughout Chadwick's work there appear rhythmic devices that clearly reflect the influence of Brahms, and Chadwick seems, by the time he composed his Third Symphony, to have gotten away from the traditional format that required a scherzo movement followed by an andante movement. Brahms did not employ either of those terms in any of his four symphonies. Chadwick had a greater preference for brass instruments than did Brahms, but their use of the remaining instruments is similar. At the deeper level of analysis, however, there are few similarities. The tonal structures of Brahms's and Chadwick's Third Symphonies are quite dissimilar, as are their melodic styles.

The symphonies of Antonin Dvořák also deserve mention for their possible influence upon Chadwick. The great Bohemian composer had come to the United States, at the urging of Jeannette Thurber (1850–1946), in 1892, to preside over the National Conservatory of Music in New York.

In the wake of his visit came greater interest in his music, much of which was already known. The Boston Symphony Orchestra had performed his symphonies as early as 1883, and his works appeared on its programs throughout the remainder of the century. Although we cannot be sure, it is certainly likely that Chadwick would have been familiar with Dvořák's Symphony No. 8 in G major, op. 88, first performed by the Boston Symphony Orchestra on February 26, 1892. Similarly, it is almost certain that Chadwick familiarized himself immediately with Dvořák's Symphony No. 9, "From the New World," op. 95, although the famous work was not performed by the Boston Symphony Orchestra until December 29, 1893.[4]

Dvořák's relationship to Brahms is well documented, and many stylistic characteristics overlap between the music of these two and Chadwick's music, including lean, classically oriented orchestration, and the use of traditional forms and harmonies. In Chadwick's Third Symphony, however, one discovers a close relationship to Dvořák that does not appear between Chadwick's symphonies and those of Brahms. In the use of sonata form, Chadwick clearly began to abandon the tonic-dominant relationship for the tonic-mediant relationship. These relationships occur in both of the symphonies by Dvořák just mentioned. In the Symphony No. 8 (mvt. 1) the principal key is G major (meas. 1), while the secondary key is B minor (meas. 77). In Dvořák's Symphony No. 9 (mvt. 1) the principal key is E minor (meas. 1), while the secondary key is G minor (meas. 91). In the fourth movement of the same work a similar tertian-relationship scheme is used; the principal key is E minor (meas. 1), and the secondary key is G major (meas. 93).

The appearance of pentatonicism in Chadwick's symphony, addressed above, might seem at first glance to evidence a relationship to Dvořák's style, particularly in his Ninth Symphony. But as we have already seen in the case of the Second Symphony, Chadwick composed pentatonic melodies long before Dvořak composed his famous work.

ANALYSIS

Movement 1

The first movement of Chadwick's Symphony No. 3, marked "Allegro sostenuto," is in sonata form (see Diagram 3–1).

Diagram 3–1. Formal Structure of First Movement.

	Intro.		Part 1 Section 1									
Theme:	O		P					P^1				t
Key:	F:I	Aug^6	I	V	V^7/A	V/V	V$^4_2$	I	a	c	a	g:V
MM.:	1	4	5	13	19	23	30	36	42	48	50	52
Comment:												

Theme:		T					(S)	
Key:		B^b———	A	vii$^{06}_5$	V	Aug^6	a	V^7/C:
MM.:	56	61	62	67	68	71	72	79
Comment:	Chad. trans.						foreshadow of S	

	Part 1 Section 2							
Theme:	S					K		
Key:	I	V	e^b	V	V$^4_3$/V	V/vi	vi—	vi
MM.:	80	87	93	98	103	107	111	113
Comment:								

Theme:							(S)
Key:			ii^{ø7}	V	I	I	I
MM.:	116	122	127	134	135	145	153
Comment:	dotted rhythms	hem.					

	Part 2 Section 3									
Theme:			T			N	(T)		P	
Key:	I	A	D$^{b6}_4$	E	G	E	B	E	a	d
MM.:	161	165	169	175	181	185	191	195	199	205
Comment:										

Theme:					(S)	K		(P)		
Key:	E	G	c	A^b	A^b	e^b	C:I	I	g	ii
MM.:	211	219	223	225	227	235	244	248	256	262
Comment:										

				Part 2 Section 4						
Theme:	S			P		(P)				
Key:	Bb:ii^{o7}	V^7———		—I	IV$^6_4$		I	c	g	D
MM.:	264	266	275	276	282	283	285	288	291	294
Comment:		Chad. trans.				horn solo				

Theme:		(S)		S	(S)			K	(S)	
Key:	Aug^6	d	F:V	I	f	V	V^7/V	A	I	Aug^6
MM.:	302	304	311	312	320	330	335	339	344	357
Comment:							hem.			

									Coda	
Theme:				(S)						
Key:	g	V	I		Aug^6	I	iv	I	I	V
MM.:	359	366	367	374	375	377	384	385	393	402
Comment:				trpt. solo						

Theme:		T		(P)	
Key:	vi	I	V^7	I———	—I
MM.:	403	409	418	420	428
Comment:					

The composition begins with four introductory measures that, as mentioned previously, can be closely linked to the ominous block-chord opening of Brahms's Third Symphony. Brahms's opening begins with a tonic chord that progresses to a diminished-seventh chord while the Chadwick opening moves from the tonic to a German-sixth chord. That leads into measure 5, where the theme associated with the principal key begins in the first violins. This theme is among Chadwick's most sweeping melodic gestures (Example 1). It displays a predilection for syncopation and

Example 1. Symphony in F (No. 3), mvt. 1, meas. 4–10.

rhythmic variety by alternately emphasizing duple and triple subdivisions of the quarter note. A variation of the main theme (P^1) occurs in measure 36 and quickly leads to the transitional area in measure 52. In measures 56–57 the favorite transitional technique is played by the upper strings. This "Chadwickian transition" consists of moving from one section to the next by employing strings (and sometimes woodwinds) in rapid scalar passages.

After a brief journey through B-flat major and A major, the theme associated with the secondary key appears in measure 72. It is presented by the horns in the key of A minor. The appearance of this theme at this point, before the secondary section proper is reached, creates an interesting problem in sonata form. The effect that should be met with the arrival of the secondary theme in the dominant key is diminished by the foreshadowing in A minor by the horns. Chadwick probably borrowed this technique from Beethoven, who employed it in his Symphony No. 3 in E flat major, op. 55 ("Eroica"). Beethoven's symphony featured a statement by the horn of a fragment of the principal theme in an anticipation of the recapitulation (meas. 394). The sounding of this theme heightens the dramatic impact of the recapitulation (meas. 398) when it is finally encountered.

The secondary section, in the dominant, occurs in measure 80. The theme associated with the dominant is a lilting melody presented, again, in the violins (Example 2).

The amount of development in this section is somewhat surprising. In the short span of 80 measures, the music modulates frequently and employs many of the themes in fragmentation. The music moves briefly through C minor (meas. 88), E-flat minor (meas. 93), and A major/minor (meas. 107–111). There is a great deal of fragmentation of the secondary theme at this point, and it occurs throughout the texture. A long hemiola section begins in measure 103, and leads into the closing theme at measure 107, which takes the music to the end of Section 2.

Example 2. Symphony in F (No. 3), mvt. 1, meas. 80–87.

The development section begins in measure 161. It marks a significant step in Chadwick's ability to develop his ideas. Here the composer manipulated themes and harmonies more freely and with greater ability than had been the case previously; similarly, he demonstrates greater control of rhythm and masterful orchestration. This area represents one of Chadwick's boldest efforts. The section begins in C major but just a few bars later, in measure 169, modulates to D-flat major. The theme used in this section is the transitional melody employed earlier (cf. meas. 61). Beginning with the oboe, it passes quickly throughout the woodwind section before it is fragmented and developed. The D-flat tonal area is followed by a rapid succession of keys that do not show evidence of any sort of planned order; on the contrary, the whole seems rather chaotic.

Firm ground is reached only at measure 244, where C major returns. There is a return of the first principal theme in measure 248, and shortly thereafter a return of the secondary theme, in measure 264, now in the key of B-flat major. At measure 266 another Chadwickian transition occurs, leading directly into section 4.

The recapitulation begins not in the tonic but rather in the key of B-flat major. There is further exploration of subdominant relationships when the music moves to the subdominant of B flat in measure 282. A horn solo based on the main theme appears in measure 283, followed by echoes in the oboe and second horn parts. In measure 304 the secondary theme is once again foreshadowed, this time in the woodwinds in D minor. The music progresses to F major in measure 311, followed by the secondary theme in measure 312.

Beginning in measure 320 there is significant development, particularly of the secondary theme. The development consists mostly of pitting various groups against one another, each playing fragments of the theme. The oboes and horns begin (meas. 320), followed by bassoons and clarinets (meas. 325), then horns and trumpets (meas. 330). Although the section does not exhibit Chadwick's considerable harmonic ingenuity (it is rather conservative), it is a good example of the composer's interest in developing the recapitulation. Here one finds large sections of hemiola (meas. 335–338), sudden rhythmic shifts (meas. 353–359), and other standard development techniques.

The coda arrives at measure 393, presenting new melodic material in the upper strings. The music associated with transitional passages (cf. meas. 62) appears in measure 409. After an echo of the theme in the horns (meas. 413), the music proceeds to a final hint of the principal theme (meas. 420), eight measures from the end of the movement.

Movement 2

The second movement of the Third Symphony, "Andante cantabile," begins with the strings in the key of B-flat major. The movement is a simple three-part structure with coda (see Diagram 3–2).

Diagram 3–2. Formal Structure of Second Movement.

	Part 1										
Theme:	A										
Key:	B^{b}:I	I	I	V^{4}_{2}	I^{6}	E^{b}:$vii^{\o 6}_{5}$	I	V	I	B^{b}:V	Aug^{6}
MM.:	1	4	9	15	16	19	22	25	28	33	34
Comment:											

					Part 2							
Theme:					B							
Key:	I^{6}	IV	V	I	b^{b}:i	e	i	Aug^{6}	D^{b6}_{4}	Aug^{6}	V^{6}_{4}	vi^{7}
MM.:	35	39	42	43	45	49	53	56	57	60	61	63
Comment:												

Theme:				B							
Key:	V	i	V/V	f:i	c	g	d	vii^{o7}/C	V^{7}	B^{6}_{4}	V/B
MM.:	67	69	83	84	88	92	96	99	100	104	110
Comment:				(circle of fifths)							

					Part 3					
Theme:					A					
Key:	B	B^{b}:IV^{6}_{4}	ii^{6}	V	I	V	IV	V^{7}/IV	IV	V^{7}
MM.:	112	113	114	116	121	135	142	146	147	155
Comment:										

					Coda			
Theme:								
Key:	I	ii^{6}	V	I	vii^{07}/d	V/^{b}VI	^{b}VI	N^{6}_{4}
MM.:	156	159	161	162	164	175	176	178
Comment:					B^{b} ped.			

Theme:					
Key:	I	IV	Aug^6	I———	I
MM.:	179	186	190	191	193
Comment:					

Part 1 begins immediately in measure 1 with a lovely, expressive, and densely harmonized melody in $\frac{3}{8}$ (Example 3). Here Chadwick exploited the string timbres to obtain a thick, rich sound. After opening in B-flat major, the music moves into the subdominant, E flat, in measure 19, but returns to B flat in measure 33. Part 2, beginning in measure 45, introduces the contrasting theme, which is found in the cellos and basses, now in B-flat minor. The material of this section is particularly Brahmsian in its design. It is highly contrapuntal and includes several additive constructions, where a figure begins in the basses and is built upon gradually in the other parts (meas. 47–48).

The second part takes the developmental role in the movement. The passage moves through E minor (meas. 49), and D-flat major (meas. 57), before modulating to F minor (meas. 84), where the secondary theme is once again restated. At this point the music moves backward through the circle of fifths, from F to C minor

Example 3. Symphony in F (No. 3), mvt. 2, meas. 1–9.

(meas. 88), G minor (meas. 92), and D minor (meas. 96), where a large, chromatic, linear-descent bass line occurs. The key of B flat finally arrives by measure 113.

Part 3 begins in measure 121 with a restatement of the material from Part 1. Here the main theme is stated by the second violins and violas, while the first violins play an obbligato part marked "espressivo."

The subdominant returns in measures 142–147, and after an authentic cadence in measures 161–162 the coda begins in measure 164 on a diminished-seventh chord. Chadwick treats the coda in an experimental way, employing sonorities that he had not previously used in the movement, including the flat VI (meas. 176) and the Neapolitan six-four (meas. 178). The movement draws to a close in one of the composer's most poignant passages. The strings begin softly in measure 184 and build quickly to forte two measures later. Here the horns assert themselves as the strings gradually move into a higher tessitura. A dramatic and unusual augmented-sixth chord appears in measure 190. While it is a subdominant construction, this chord is not of the German or Italian type; rather it is a minor sonority with an augmented sixth. It leads to the quiet final measures in B-flat major.

Movement 3

Like the second movement of this symphony, the third comprises a clearly articulated three-part form (see Diagram 3–3).

Diagram 3–3. Formal Structure of Third Movement.

	Part 1											
Theme:	A							B/A				
Key:	d:i	i	VI	N	VI	V^6/III	III^6	i	i	iv	N^6	V^6
MM.:	1	5	9	10	14	16	20	21	25	29	33	39
Comment:								Pentatonic				

Theme:		T									B/A
Key:	i	V	V	$vii^{\circ 6}_{5}$/V	IV	V/V	a	i	$vii^{\circ 7}$	i——	—i
MM.:	40	41	47	50	53	62	68	74	77	80	98
Comment:											

				Part 2					
Theme:				C					
Key:	i	VI	i	D:I	I	d	^{b}VI	V/^{b}VI	V^{7}
MM.:	102	108	117	118	129	130	133	134	138
Comment:									

								Part 3		
Theme:								A		
Key:	V	I	vi	I	V^{7}–I	vi	I	d:i	a	VI
MM.:	141	153	156	164	168	169	177	178	195	203
Comment:										

Theme:							B/A	
Key:	V$^{4}_{3}$/E^{b}	E^{b}	F	G	vii^{o7}/C	vii^{o7}/D	Aug^{6}	V$^{4}_{3}$/E^{b}
MM.:	208	209	211	213	215	216	217	218
Comment:								

Theme:		B/A					B			
Key:	VI	V	i	N	B^{b6}	V	i	VI	VI	V^{7}
MM.:	224	225	229	233	239	244	245	258	265	272
Comment:										

	Coda							
Theme:	A					C	A	
Key:	i	I	I	VI$^{6}_{4}$	VI$^{6}_{4}$	I	I	I
MM.:	273	277	294	303	310	315	333	339
Comment:		D pedal						

Part 1 begins in the key of D minor. The first theme is heard immediately in the first bar in the second violins (Example 4). It is a quick-moving melody that progresses through the submediant and the Neapolitan within the first 10 bars, as if in imitation of the coda section of the previous movement. Here Chadwick created unity

Example 4. Symphony in F (No. 3), mvt. 3, meas. 1–6.

between movements based on sonority rather than on theme, and exploited the closeness of the B flat of the previous movement and the D minor of the present movement.

The second theme of the first part is heard in measure 21 in the horns. This theme, in duple meter, is a slower-moving melody, which is soon echoed in the flutes (meas. 25). Throughout this part the first violins play the first theme as a countermelody. A long transitional passage begins in measure 41. At measure 98 the two melodic ideas are heard simultaneously again, just before the close of the part in measure 117.

Part 2 begins in measure 118 in D major. The main theme in this section is a folklike melody introduced by the horns. By virtue of its employment of an initial leap of a perfect fifth as well as its general contour, the theme is closely related to the second theme of Part 1.

After passing briefly through D minor in measure 130, the music progresses through B-flat major (meas. 133). Most of the thematic material in this part is based on the theme encountered earlier (cf. meas. 118). After the dominant is reached in measure 138, the theme begins to dissipate, not re-forming until measure 153. The theme, in the tonic, gradually crescendos to its climax in measures 162–168. A brief transitional passage, characterized by diminishing figures in the low tessitura of the strings, leads to the next section.

Part 3 returns to the key of D minor, with the first theme sounded in measure 178. It is the most developmental part of this movement thus far. The music moves at various points through A minor (meas. 195), B-flat major (meas. 203), E-flat major (meas. 209), F major (meas. 211), and G major (meas. 213). The two themes of Part 1 are once again juxtaposed in measure 217 and remain important thematic ideas until the coda is reached in measure 273. In the coda, considerable harmonic weight falls on B-flat major (meas. 303–310), but as the end of the work nears there is a return to the theme of Part 2 in measure 315, as the movement closes in D major.

Movement 4

The finale of Chadwick's Third Symphony is marked "Allegro molto energico." It is in sonata form, although it is a somewhat shorter structure than might be expected for this symphony's final movement (see Diagram 3–4).

Diagram 3–4. Formal Structure of Fourth Movement.

			Part 1 Section 1								
Theme:			P							t	
Key:	F:	V	I	V	V/E^b:	I	V^6/F:	V^7	I	V——	—V^9/V
MM.:		1	3	11	14	15	22	27	28	36	53
Comment:											

		Part 1 Section 2				
Theme:		S				
Key:	vii^o/V	C:I	I	c:iv–V–i	d:iv–V–i	e:iv–V–i
MM.:	54	58	66	70	72	74
Comment:						

										Part 2 Section 3	
Theme:			k				(P)				
Key:	E^b	vii^{o7}/C:	I	I	ii	I	I	F:	V^7	I	f
MM.:	81	85	87	95	99	105	113		117	121	126
Comment:											

Theme:			S				S			
Key:	E	A	d		f	G^b	V/V	V	V	I
MM.:	130	134	138	142	146	150	154	157	169	178
Comment:										

		Part 2 Section 4								
Theme:		P						(P)		
Key:	V	F:I	V	I	I^6_4	g	E	f	E^b	vii^{o7}/B^b:
MM.:	185	193	201	204	205	209	211	215	219	221
Comment:										

Theme:	S							
Key:	I	V	I	V/V	V	V^4_3/b^b	f:iv–V–i	g:iv–V–i
MM.:	228	230	231	235	236	239	240	242
Comment:								

								Coda 1	
Theme:								P	
Key:	a:iv–V–i	A$^{\flat}$	V/F:	I	vii$^{\circ 4}_{3}$	$^{\flat}$VI^{6}	Aug^{6}	I$^{6}_{4}$	V
MM.:	244	251	255	257	259	261	264	265	274
Comment:								$\frac{6}{4}$	

	Coda 2		Coda 3				Coda 4		
Theme:	t						S		
Key:	I	Aug^{6}	V$^{6}_{4}$/iii	V/vi	vi	V	I	I	iii
MM.:	275	290	291	293	311	318	319	322	325
Comment:							$\frac{1}{1}$		

Theme:		(P)					
Key:	V/E$^{\flat}$	F:IV	Aug^{6}	I	I–V	I———	I
MM.:	332	345	352	353	357	361	369
Comment:							

After two introductory measures on the dominant, the music progresses swiftly to the first statement of the theme associated with the principal key. It is a sprightly, joyous melody, played fortissimo by the horns (Example 5). The music moves briefly through E-flat major (meas. 15) and quickly progresses to the dominant of F major in measure 22.

An unexpected interruption occurs in measure 28, where the music shifts abruptly into $\frac{4}{4}$ meter. While it remains in F major, its style and melodic material are new. Especially noteworthy is Chadwick's reliance on the trumpet. Here the instrument receives a degree of exposure that it seldom gets in a symphony, in a fanfarelike flourish. The section lasts only eight measures before moving on to the transition (meas. 36).

Example 5. Symphony in F (No. 3), mvt. 4, meas. 3–6.

The secondary area is reached in measure 58, where the key of C major arrives. The secondary theme is a lovely "romance," a gently flowing melody in four-bar phrases marked "largamente" and found in the lower register of the upper strings. This "romance" style of writing became increasingly characteristic of Chadwick's slower movements; generally speaking, the style is lyrical and sentimental, without the drama and pathos that is often typical of slower symphonic movements, although a good deal of development occurs.

Chadwick took the opportunity to develop the secondary material more than usual in this section. In fact, the development of this material begins almost immediately after its first statement. In measure 70 a sequential progression begins, through C minor (meas. 70), D minor (meas. 72), and E minor (meas. 74), eventually progressing to E-flat major (meas. 81). After the presentation of material borrowed from the opening in measure 85, the closing section is reached at measure 87, once again in the key of C major. The section comes to a close in measure 120.

The development begins in measure 121 in F major. The section presents a fragment of the principal theme, sounded in the oboe, and then the material begins to fragment even more and spread throughout the orchestra. Almost immediately in this "fantasy" section, the music begins to explore numerous tonalities in rapid succession. Between measure 121 and measure 138 the music touches on F major, F minor, E major, A major, and D minor, respectively. At measure 138 the secondary theme forms the subject for a fugato. The first statement of the subject occurs in the first violins, followed four measures later in the lower strings. Measure 154, marked "animato," brings the retransition to F major (signaled by a V/V) and the reappearance of the trumpet fanfare (cf. meas. 28). The section comes to an end after the dominant is reached (meas. 185–192).

The recapitulation presents the theme associated with the principal key, again in the horn (meas. 193). In this section, as in the recapitulations of Chadwick's earlier symphony movements, there is a good deal of development. There are excursions through several tonalities before the secondary theme enters in measure 228. Here, however, the music is in B flat, the subdominant, rather than the expected tonic. Throughout this section, too, there is a great deal of development before the return to F major in measure 257.

The first of four sections of the coda begins in measure 265. As is typical of Chadwick's codas, this one is multi-sectional, in a different style from the rest of the work and in a different meter, with new melodic material. In this coda, Chadwick employed (although only briefly) many of the themes presented earlier in the movement. The first section presents material associated with the principal key, while the second section (meas. 275) features transitional material (cf. meas. 36). The third section of the coda (meas. 291) presents the theme associated with the principal key in the trumpet part, while the secondary theme is presented in augmentation in the upper woodwinds. The final section, marked "presto" (meas. 319), presents material derived from the secondary theme in the lower woodwinds and the upper strings. The subdominant is reached in measure 345, where the trumpet sounds a fanfare figure based on the principal theme. The movement ends in rousing fashion in the tonic key.

CRITICAL RECEPTION

Critics by no means agreed on either the quality or the substance of Chadwick's Third Symphony. Although it had won first prize in a competition overseen by Dvořak, who was at the time idolized by American concertgoers, not all critics responded positively to Chadwick's efforts. In fact, notably few reviewers found this work entirely satisfactory. The critic for the *Boston Evening Transcript* was overwhelmingly pleased, stating sardonically,

> Mr. Chadwick's new symphony has won a success with both musicians and the public that augurs well for its future life. Indeed, as prize symphonies go, one wonders a little how so fine a work should have won a prize.[5]

The critic went on to cite what he claimed was an old saying among Viennese musicians, which essentially notes that symphonies that win prizes end up with a short history. But then he noted that "it would take something more than a prize to kill this symphony!"[6] In an astoundingly technical analysis, the reviewer pointed out what he believed to be a humorous discrepancy in its use of traditional symphonic language, the employment of the "musical joke" of fooling the listener into thinking that the saltarello theme (meas. 1) of the third movement is the principal theme, when in fact the reviewer believed the countermelody (meas. 21) to be the main theme. (The present study has, in fact, concluded that the saltarello theme is indeed the principal theme.)

Having noted this irregularity, the critic went on to write that

> The form of the symphony is strictly regular and orthodox; and one finds this regularity of form all the more admirable, and in no wise open [*sic*] to the charge of mere scholasticism, in that it plainly springs from the way in which Mr. Chadwick has here confined himself to the coherent and musically logical development and work[ing] out of his thematic subject matter, without allowing himself any of that sort of capricious musical skylarking for which he has on some other occasions shown considerable inclination. In this symphony the composer has kept his seriousness throughout, as he did in his "Melpomene" overture; and he has lost not a whit of his native charm and fascination by so doing.[7]

Finally, after several lines of encomia, the reviewer sums up Chadwick's achievement:

> That Mr. Chadwick has succeeded in carrying the larger form as high as he did the smaller is quite enough to his credit, and shows no inconsiderable advance beyond his former, already high, position.[8]

The great music critic Philip Hale, who had already written about Chadwick's Second Symphony, was also in attendance at the premiere of the Third Symphony. While he always seems to have had many kind words to say about the composer and his works, the present composition generally did not please him. Hale began with thoughts about Chadwick:

> It is not necessary to tell the story of Mr. Chadwick's career. He is not a man of promise, he is a man of actual performance. Whether you look at the "Melpomene" overture, the piano quintet, or the "Phoenix Expirans," you acknowledge gladly a talent that at times almost suggests genius.[9]

This wonderful paragraph is quickly followed by an unenthusiastic review of the work:

> But to me at least this symphony was a disappointment. Everywhere is there evidence of labor, thoughtfulness, sincerity and nobility of aim. I do not find, however, the spontaneity, the warm and sensuous coloring, the homogeneity that characterize his best work even when it is of small proportions.
>
> As you know, this symphony was awarded the prize offered by the National Conservatory of Music. The fact alone that a symphony won a prize does not inspire confidence. There's that long-winded geographical, anthropological and historical thing by Raff, to take an example. Even a jury of professors may go astray, be frightened by the boldness or arrogance of deserving youth, be flattered by humble imitation of their own works, or complimented by evident respect paid their choicest theories. The prize piece may be either hopelessly academic or of flagrant originality. The road to the Temple of Fame is paved with prize compositions trodden under foot, forgotten by the cutthroat band that rush toward the closed door.
>
> But this symphony by Mr. Chadwick does not openly suffer from its association with a prize. It is not academic in the sense that much of the music of Villiers-Stanford, Foote, [and] Mackenzie is academic. Nor on the other hand is there a wild desire to bombard the firmament with rockets.[10]

Hale's preceding paragraphs say more about his own position regarding composition contests than anything else, and his insight into the motives of juries and their biases is keen. The critic quickly got to the point of his above statements:

> Mr. Chadwick has been sitting at the feet of Mr. Johannes Brahms. He has also listened—no doubt unconsciously—to the pleasing performance of Mr. Anton Dvorak [*sic*] on the celebrated instrument known as the Negro-Indian American pipe, which I believe is the invention of Messrs. Krehbiel & Company. Not that he has in any degree whatever copied either of these men. The feeling, the mood, however, of the first movement and the finale is Brahmsian. The scherzo contains a theme, first given out by a horn, which resembles the true Negro-American tune; it is not a Bohemian melody,

> strengthened or diluted, as you please, with Glenlivet for domestic use in Spillville, Ia. As I wrote in another newspaper, "The theme has a popular character that in the absence of a more precise phrase may be described as a folk song or wandering melody that is repeated by a negro, and undergoes modifications without the specific intent of the dusky singer. It has the true mixture of reckless indifference and superficial melancholy." So again the scherzo is in the "American" mode of Dvorak [*sic*]. But Mr. Chadwick has avoided the mistake of trying deliberately to turn a serious work of art into a wandering booth where alleged folk songs are labeled and pointed out by the stick of the showman.[11]

It is somewhat difficult to know what to make of these comments. While he accused Chadwick of "sitting at the feet" of Brahms, and of having some knowledge of Dvořák's work, Hale denied that Chadwick copied them in any way. Surely the author meant that, without borrowing specific ideas from either of the great European composers, Chadwick had emulated their general style in his Third Symphony. The foregoing analysis has shown, however, that Chadwick had, in fact, borrowed specific ideas from both composers. Perhaps after a single hearing Hale was not able to identify Chadwick's ideas as having originated with Brahms and Dvořák; one wonders, though, how he could possibly have missed references to Brahms's Third Symphony in the opening bars of the composition.

Hale proceeded to elaborate upon specific complaints:

> The first movement, an allegro sostenuto, suffers from the desire of the composer to give out a great amount of musical information. I admire his patience, and I admire the strength of certain passages, although the impression of the movement was one of technical proficiency rather than of invention of color. The movement is prolix, and the speaker at times hems and haws. More popular undoubtedly will be the second movement, a larghetto in B flat major, in which there is a tunefulness; in which there is a more genuine passion than in the allegro that preceded. After one hearing the scherzo seemed to me the most characteristic and musical movement of the symphony. It is not so "intellectual," and perhaps for that reason may be only tolerated by those to whom the mission of music is to produce a knitting together

> of the eyebrows. But I recognize in it the man I know, the sane, humorous, brusque, imaginative, highly endowed Yankee. The finale shares with this scherzo the glory of the work. I like the broad and flowing second theme, the dramatic effects of the syncopation. Yet other passages in this finale seemed dull and unnecessarily noisy.[12]

Again, it is in the composition of the scherzo, lighthearted music that is generally skillfully orchestrated, that the composer garners the most praise. Much as he seems to have tried to create dramatic works exuding depth and substance throughout his career, particularly in his symphonies, Chadwick simply had few successes, at least to judge by the critical reviews. Perhaps the most surprising comment in the above paragraph is that Hale did not like the finale; Chadwick's spectacular endings were usually appreciated by the critics.

Hale finally concluded his review with more general and vague complaints. Although a few of his words are kind, particularly as regards sections of Chadwick's orchestration, some of the less favorable comments are hidden among Hale's own brand of poetic criticism:

> In this symphony the modulations are often like an invitation given in dreams to climb a little higher to see the offered prospect; but these modulations prepare too often for disappointment; the view is one of commonplace, and mist enshrouds it. Mr. Chadwick, on the other hand, has been most fortunate in suggesting, and by apparently simple means, the thought of mystery, as in the first movement by a use of horns and clarinets. The symphony is strong in the matter of rhythm, occasionally too strong, as when rhythm is tortured till it shrieks.
>
> Much of the instrumentation seemed over studied, themes without contrast [*sic*]. Mr. Chadwick in this work has displayed a passion for horns that is almost frenetic, and one is tempted to try a homeopathic remedy and ward off evil by the finger horn of Italy.[13]

Another review of the premiere performance of the Third Symphony, written by another well-known critic, Louis C. Elson, begins with the headline "Mr. Chadwick's Ambitious Work Heard." Before a discussion of Chadwick's composition, the critic wrote of his pleasure that, at last, an American work was being performed:

> While one may be thoroughly averse to pampering the American muse, by giving concerts of native compositions, as such, yet it would be much worse to discriminate against the native school, and to confine the repertoire to European works, as was done at one stage in the history of these concerts. One may commend Mr. [Emil] Paur's catholicity of taste and predict that the public will be the gainers by it.[14]

The hopes raised for a good review of the symphony by Elson's praising of the concept of the concert are quickly dashed by his thoughts on the composition:

> When Mr. Chadwick came upon the stage to direct his symphony there was a most spontaneous outburst of applause; but the applause was not quite so unhesitating after the first movement had come to an end. It is a symphony in which the composer has exerted all his ingenuity, and studied from the manuscript it must contain many points of profound interest to the musician, but it is quite another matter to the auditor, who lets many a bit of augmentation, of diminution and of contrary motion slip by unperceived.[15]

Elson proceeded to make his complaints more specific:

> In the first movement the composer leads one into a development that is a jungle made up of fragments. The composer falls into the style of Brahms in giving many small thoughts rather than one continuous one, but Brahms's piece-work is the more intelligible. Nevertheless when the composer has worked his themes sufficiently to show that he is up to the symphonic standard, he becomes more natural and gives a really great climax. The end of the first movement is an instance of this. The second and third movements please the present writer best, for the Larghetto has a noble chief theme and there is good contrast in it, while the Scherzo is as dainty in its humor as if it were by that prince of scherzo-writers, Mendelssohn.[16]

One must wonder why fragments in a development were considered unusual by Elson. Yet, the pejorative judgment that his music "fell into" the style of Brahms was one that Chadwick had encountered before. Such charges make one wonder whom, if not Brahms, Elson might have considered worthy of emulation in symphonic composition. Although Mendelssohn is clearly among his favorites for works in scherzo style, the critic does not name composers whom Chadwick ought to have adopted as models. Elson's 1925 monograph *The History of American Music* provides no insight into this question; the book is primarily descriptive and neither praises nor disparages the many influences on American composers. Chadwick had often been accused of academicism, as is implied by Elson's statement that the composer "worked his themes sufficiently to show that he was up to the symphonic standard." Hale's criticisms of the Third Symphony as a prize composition immediately come to mind, although Elson did not concentrate on the fact that the work was a prizewinner.

As in other reviews, Chadwick is praised for his work in final movements, climaxes, and scherzos, and is even compared to the acknowledged master, Mendelssohn. Elson, too, had kind words to say about the slow movement, an area where Chadwick is not often praised. Elson completed his review by stating,

> All in all, one finds much to praise in the work, but at the end must confess that the great American symphony is not yet written. Mr. Chadwick directed the orchestra with much steadiness and discretion.[17]

Yet another critic, Warren Davenport, was unimpressed by the symphony. After admitting that it is difficult to assess the value of the work after a single hearing, he went on to explain,

> One is induced to conclude that Mr. Chadwick has failed to achieve a success. That there are places in the composition that are agreeable, when compared with the cast of the rest of the work, cannot be denied; but, as a whole, the music is labored and dry; the themes lack nobility; the thematic development is disappointing; the ideas advanced are without purpose, or over-elaborated and weighted [*sic*] down with a loud and noisy orchestration; the progressions in the wind passages are often discordant and ear-splitting in their violence and are not mollified in the least by the efforts of the strings, which are employed also with an overabundance of vigor, at times, while the whole work moves on in patches,

> incoherent and obscure, as regards true musical form, if that is the composer's intention. There are contrasts to be sure, but in no marked degree—not enough to relieve the monotone of a want of color, through the absence of nuances to make expressive each movement in itself, to say nothing of the general monotone of similarity, as regards effects, that runs through the work as a whole.[18]

Chadwick had rarely encountered such remarks. Although by now the composer was no stranger to poor reviews and, no doubt, frequently dismissed them, Davenport's summation was particularly vicious. In retrospect, several of the charges lack merit. Admittedly, some of the themes are weak and the development in certain areas is predictable, but Chadwick's vivid orchestration is often superb; he had a wonderful ear for tone coloring and an expert's knowledge of what orchestral instruments were capable of displaying.

Davenport did not entirely separate his review of the performance from a review of the work. On the contrary, many of his thoughts about the latter were based upon weaknesses of the former. One gets the idea that the orchestra was an unbridled group, uninterested in dynamic markings and unable to control their instruments. "Loud and noisy orchestration," passages "ear-splitting in their violence," and "an overabundance of vigor" may easily have been faults of the performance, not the work. This fact is corroborated by Hale's earlier remark that the finale was "unnecessarily noisy."

The critic continued to levy his attack in a manner that suggests that he was philosophically opposed to music competitions, when he continued,

> It does not seem that Mr. Chadwick had been warmed to his work by the divine spark when he wrote this symphony. Mr. Chadwick is a good musician and has had ample training in his art, and it seems as if these factors had come to his aid in competing for the prize rather than any fertility of invention or spontaneity that could arise from inspiration alone.
>
> If the masterpieces in this form of composition by Mozart, Beethoven, Schumann, Mendelssohn, Schubert, Brahms, Paine, Raff, and Dvorak [*sic*] are symphonies, then this work of Mr. Chadwick's must be placed in some other class of composition.

> It may be that in the course of writing for a prize, where one screws their courage up to a certain musical sticking point and lets knowledge and labor serve their purpose instead of knowledge and inspiration, may be accountable for the effort Mr. Chadwick has made in this case [*sic*].[19]

The critic's disparaging diatribe was not over. Davenport went on to attack other aspects of Chadwick's musicianship when he stated,

> Mr. Chadwick conducted his work on this occasion, but it would have been better had he set [*sic*] apart and listened to the results of his labor, trusting its performance in the hands of Mr. Paur, who would have perhaps, made clearer what was so obscure under Mr. Chadwick's baton, for throughout the playing it was marked by coarseness in the execution and the want of contrast. As for nuances and repose, they were conspicuous by their absence.
>
> To be a good musician and beat in time is one thing, but to conduct and bring forth in its best light an intricate composition is quite another thing.[20]

Thus earlier comments regarding the effects of the performance on the critic's perception of the composition ultimately lead one to suspect that Chadwick himself deserves the blame for the supposedly ungracious orchestration of the symphony. Chadwick often conducted his own compositions and was frequently lauded for his fine work on the podium; it has already been noted in this study that he harbored notions of conducting professionally during the early stages of his career. Apparently the various music directors of the Boston Symphony Orchestra, where so many of his works were premiered, must have had a great deal of faith in his abilities with the baton to allow Chadwick such an honor. Whether or not it was really a good idea, at least with the Third Symphony, is another matter. The work surpasses the First and Second Symphonies in its dramatic content and would therefore have required a good deal more from its conductor than its predecessors. Whether or not Chadwick should have conducted at this performance is difficult to judge; the poor reviews certainly did not deter him from future conducting endeavors.

One of the least critical articles regarding the Third Symphony comes from a review, apparently of an 1896 concert held in upstate New York, in the *Buffalo Express*. Quoted in another newspaper, the review reads as follows:

> After listening to this composition who shall say that there is no creative musical art in America? Greater symphonies have been written, no doubt, but this one is masterful, musicianly, thoroughly original and strikingly attractive, and reflects credit upon the land which produced it. If anyone sought to find anything distinctively American about this composition, he must have been disappointed. It was what might be called a cosmopolitan symphony, one that would sound as fitting in Munich as in Buffalo, in Paris as in London. Mr. Chadwick was himself and no one else. The leading melodies were always attractive; that of the andante was surpassingly beautiful. The thought is well sustained and well worked out. In this composition Mr. Chadwick showed a command of the wonderful resources of tone painting contained in a full orchestra, but did not allow himself to be betrayed into excessive elaboration. The first movement was solid and well considered, the third vivacious and the fourth a good ending of the symphony; but probably no one will deny that the second, the andante, touched him more than any of the others. A melody, tender and sweet, is given out, first by the strings and then swelled to fullness by the other choirs of the orchestra. It was full of fine feeling and eloquent expression.[21]

Although the identity of the author is unknown, as are his qualifications as a music critic, it is at least notable that several of the same themes that have already been sounded, including Chadwick's ability as an orchestrator and finale composer, are noted here.

In 1904 the Boston Symphony Orchestra performed an all-Chadwick concert, no doubt as a tribute to his considerable output and achievements on behalf of native music in Boston and the United States. The Third Symphony was included on the program and performed last. The character of this review of the symphony, written 10 years after the work's premiere, is markedly different from many of the comments that followed the first performance:

> The first movement of this is full of learned musicianship, the development of themes being the most carefully carried

> out that we know of in any American instrumental work. Yet we admire the grandeur of the climax more than the ingenuity of the thematic treatment; it is more spontaneous and poetic. Mr. Chadwick gives a nobility of theme to the Larghetto that deserves recognition; there is a loftiness to this part of the work, that makes it very impressive. In Scherzo we think this composer is emphatically the American master; no one can rival him in his playful and rollicking touches.[22]

There are several reasons for the tameness of this review. First of all, tributes lead necessarily to complimenting the person being honored. Critics risk being accused of poor taste if they see fit to attack established personages. Perhaps at this juncture in his life, Chadwick would have been better served by a more scathing review, one that would have indicated that his works were vital and important. Unfortunately, as the composer probably realized, tributes are often commemorative, celebrations of one's accomplishments in the past. It is not unreasonable to suggest that Chadwick had lived on into a time in which his works were no longer considered relevant. Certainly, the symphony as a genre did not hold the position of esteem that it did when the Yankee was a youth. This leads to the second possible reason that the review lacked serious criticism: that the work did not really matter. The symphony was "nice," as Charles Ives might have said, a bit old-fashioned, couched in ideas and styles that belonged to an earlier age. We can be fairly certain that by 1904 many would have considered the symphony a leftover from a bygone era, an academic effort by an esteemed American "professor."

Perhaps Chadwick's disappointment with many of the reviews was tempered the next year when he read a review from Leipzig, which had been reprinted in the *Boston Globe*. The review, written by Paul Zschörlich and appearing in 1905, has since become one of the most famous articles in Chadwick research. In it the critic pointed out the fine qualities in the composition, stating,

> I declare that I consider this symphony the best of all that have been written since Brahms. It is extraordinarily rich in tone color and masterly in construction and instrumentation. It is hard to say what most strongly seizes the listener—the joyous energy of the first movement, the original humor of the third, or the sturdy manliness of the last, which closes in

> such splendid pomp. The rhythmic variety, the harmonic detail, the superb tone-coloring and the wonderfully clear part-writing all demand unstinted praise. . . . [23]

As if such magnificent praise were not enough, the critic went on to write some remarkable words about the composer:

> From this symphony, I hold George W. Chadwick to be the most important living Anglo-American composer—Edward Elgar not excepted.[24]

CHAPTER 6

INTRODUCTION TO THE QUASI-SYMPHONIES

Chadwick began composing his *Symphonic Sketches* (1895–1904) in the year following the Third Symphony. This work marks an important turning point in the composer's thought about symphonic procedures. With the *Sketches,* Chadwick took leave of the abstract symphony to compose works that bear resemblance to the symphony proper in terms of form and tonal structure but that differ in that they are somewhat programmatic and not so serious in dramatic content. These "quasi-symphonies" include not only the *Symphonic Sketches,* but two other works, the *Sinfonietta* (1904) and the *Suite Symphonique* (1909).

The reasons for Chadwick's abandonment of the traditional abstract symphony can only be conjectured. Yellin has suggested several possible reasons: (1) The composer hoped to avoid comparisons of his works with other compositions called "symphonies" during a time when music critics were not sympathetic to American composers' efforts in the genre; (2) Stylistically they are not directly related to traditional symphonies, but are distinctly American; (3) Aesthetically, they are less severe in style than was expected in a symphony, perhaps intended to entertain rather than illuminate, and therefore are not completely deserving of the grandiose title "symphony."[1]

Yellin's assertions deserve some scrutiny. It seems unlikely that Chadwick would have given in to the critics of his day on matters of what he should compose. All his life he exhibited a great deal of independence and would not have been easily swayed into abandoning a genre with which he had a fair amount of success. It is true, of course, that the admiration for his Third Symphony was not universal; in a letter to Theodore Thomas (December 15,

1894), Chadwick wrote that Boston Symphony Orchestra members who premiered the symphony were "quite enthusiastic about it, which is enough to condemn it for a newspaper man."[2] The comment exhibits the composer's disdain for the press, but at the same time, he must have written these words with some degree of satisfaction; by the time he had communicated with Thomas, Chadwick had received a prize for the symphony, not to mention several good reviews, and recognition by Dvořák. In addition, by the mid–1890s Chadwick was an established figure on the American music scene and did not have to go out of his way to please the music critics.

Yellin's second point, that the quasi-symphonies are not directly related to the traditional symphony, can also be disputed. In fact, these works are very traditional in terms of their basic forms and key structures—in them can be found sonata forms, standard tonal relationships within a movement and between movements, and the usual layout of the movements (e.g., fast-slow-scherzo-fast). The works depart from the stream of traditional symphonic writing in their use of programmaticism, but this is not an innovation begun by Chadwick; similar procedures can be found rather early in symphonic history.

Finally, it is certainly possible that Chadwick, having had a rather severe musical education in Leipzig, may have felt that these rather tongue-in-cheek works did not deserve the status of a symphony. Yellin's third point, therefore, seems the most convincing of his three.

CHAPTER 7

SYMPHONIC SKETCHES

HISTORY

With the possible exception of the Second Symphony, the four movements comprising the *Symphonic Sketches* are probably Chadwick's most successful orchestral compositions. Whether the work was originally conceived as a whole is a matter of some uncertainty. The movements were composed out of their eventual published sequence; the first movement, "Jubilee," was completed on December 1, 1895; the second movement, "Noël," was completed a few days earlier, on November 21, 1895. Apparently the composer remained dedicated to this set of compositions through the beginning of the new year, for the final movement, "A Vagrom Ballad," was completed on February 13, 1896. The eventual third movement, "Hobgoblin," was not completed until February 10, 1904 however.[1] It is possible that Chadwick had originally intended to use a waltz in the *Symphonic Sketches,* for the work that was eventually titled *Everywoman Waltz* at first bore the heading *S. S. Waltz,* perhaps referring to the present work. The waltz was composed at approximately the same time as *Symphonic Sketches.*[2] The composition, dedicated to Chadwick's friend and pupil the American composer Frederick S. Converse (1871–1940), was first performed in its entirety by the Boston Symphony Orchestra on February 7, 1908.

To the beginning of each movement Chadwick added several lines of verse. Victor Yellin has written that

> Because of the evocative generic elements of the music, signalled by Chadwick's own epigraphic titles and preambular quotations, these *Sketches* must . . . be placed within the orbit of program music.[3]

There is no question but that Chadwick intended the poetry and the music to reflect a similar mood. But *Symphonic Sketches* is not actually "program music" in the more specific sense of the music following a plot. Yellin may have been more convincing had he used the term "characteristic music" to describe the work. That is, Chadwick composed music that evokes images for the listener but does not describe a particular set of circumstances. Besides the fact that the preambular poetry is brief and does not have a "plot" as such, it should be noted that we cannot be sure whether the poetry inspired the music or whether the composer simply attached the lines to the completed composition to give the listener a sense of mood. As Yellin also noted,

> The title itself is ambiguous. It may refer to literary and dramatic as well as visual arts. In the case of the first three movements or sketches . . . there is a question as to whether the composer's intention was to tell a story or paint a picture. But the last sketch, "A Vagrom Ballad," definitely may be understood only as a vaudeville or music hall act.[4]

Yellin was correct when he wrote that the title is ambiguous and that it possibly refers to one of several artistic disciplines. But the composer intended to create an intrinsically musical work, not "to tell a story or paint a picture" or even produce "a vaudeville or music hall act." In doing so, he used interesting vernacular musical materials set in traditional forms.

Yellin has discussed *Symphonic Sketches* at greater length than any of Chadwick's other symphonies. In a 1975 article, "Chadwick, American Musical Realist," he considered the Yankee master in light of the turn-of-the-century tendency toward "realism" in art.[5] In the article, he described the composition as "one of the most realistic musical works in American musical history," attributing the realism to Chadwick's employment of scenes from everyday life and to the presence of unusual musical materials, including pentatonic and modal tunes, habanera rhythm, cross accents, and brassy orchestration.[6] Yellin heartily asserted that "gone is the concern for exotica, the bizarre, or the romantic."[7]

A closer look at *Symphonic Sketches,* however, reveals quite the opposite, at least in terms of traditional symphonic composition and in terms of Chadwick's symphonic output to this point in his career. The composer's First Symphony was clearly based on classical models, and although the Second and Third Symphonies were more romantic in their method and approach, in form, rhythm, and melodic style they are classically grounded. There are slight exceptions, of course; the scherzo of the Second Symphony and some areas of the Third are notable for their use of "exotic" or unusual elements. By and large, however, they follow established conventions of symphonic composition.

Symphonic Sketches ignores much of what had come before; in the use of Afro-Caribbean rhythmic patterns, pentatonic melodies, employment of modernisms from France, humor, orchestration, overtly sentimental tunes, and innovative tonal schemes, this work is distinguishable precisely for its unconventional tendencies in a musical society that lagged somewhat behind European musical circles and that was itself still classically oriented. As Yellin stated, the work is among the most important in American musical history, but he cited the wrong reason when he noted its importance as a work of "realism."[8] In his recent monograph about Chadwick, Yellin stated that *Symphonic Sketches* does not "celebrate nostalgia for a mythic past but convey[s] the view, through Chadwick's mind, of aspects of contemporary life."[9] As noted above, the audiences of Boston would have been familiar with conservative compositions, like those of the established European masters and American composers such as John Knowles Paine and other classically trained musicians. Certainly French modernisms and habanera rhythms are exotic and would have been extremely so to contemporary audiences. Similarly, notions of "Puck," in his first sketch, and of "hobgoblins," in his third sketch, are not aspects of everyday life. Yellin tried too hard to cast the composition into the mold of realism, an artistic movement that was taking hold during the period of the work's evolution. Far from moving away from "exotica, the bizarre, and the romantic," the set of *Symphonic Sketches* might reasonably be regarded as one of the most exotic and romantic works in the American canon.

ANALYSIS

Movement 1

The first movement of *Symphonic Sketches,* subtitled "Jubilee," begins with the following verse:

No cool gray tones for me!
Give me the warmest red and green,
A cornet and a tambourine,
To paint MY Jubilee!

For when pale flutes and oboes play,
to sadness I become a prey;
Give me the violets and the May,
But no gray skies for me!

The composition opens in A major without an introduction. It is a large sonata form but includes several unusual twists, which make it one of Chadwick's most original works (see Diagram 4–1).

Diagram 4–1. Formal Structure of "Jubilee."

	Part 1 Section 1					
Theme:	P	P	P			
Key:	A:I	iii	V^6_4		Aug^6———	I
MM.:	1	9	17	24	26	27
Comment:	$\frac{6}{4}$			hemiola		

Theme:	T	T			
Key:	iii	g#:i	E:V^7	I	V/C
MM.:	28	35	42	48	54
Comment:	$\frac{4}{4}$	seq.	frags.		

	Section 2					Part 2 Section 3
Theme:	S^1	S^2				t
Key:	C:I		I	V	I	F-B^b-E^{b7}-A^b/G#
MM.:	58	63	72	93	94	96
Comment:	horn call					

						Section 4	
Theme:	P		P	S^1	T		
Key:	c#:i^6_4	D:I	E:I^6_4	V	I	V/A:I——	I
MM.:	110	118	122	126	145	157	185
Comment:	$\frac{6}{4}$				frags.		

Theme:	S^1	S^2			t	
Key:	F:I	I	V^7	I	V–I	F–B^{b7}–E^b–A^b–D^b/$C^{\#}$
MM.:	186	191	199	206	221	222
Comment:						

	Coda 1			Coda 2		Coda 3
Theme:	(P)		P	N		S^2
Key:	V/f$^{\#}$:i	Aug^6	A:I^6_4	V	D^b($C^{\#}$)	
MM.:	238		250	254	273	274
Comment:				ferm.	frag.	

	Coda 4		Coda 5	
Theme:				
Key:	I	IV	I	I
MM.:	282	314	315	333
Comment:			Presto	

A jubilant theme, marked "Allegro molto vivace," begins in measure 1 (Example 1). The character of the theme, played by the upper woodwinds and upper strings is reminiscent of a fanfare; it is rhythmically solid, and a flourish links its phrases (meas. 8, 16). At measure 9 the theme is heard again, this time transposed up a major third, and at measure 17 it sounds again, this time on the dominant. Such harmonic movement from tonic to mediant and then to dominant has not been encountered previously in the present study. A passage of hemiola occurs beginning in measure 24 and serves to articulate the new meter, $\frac{4}{4}$, which begins in measure 28. This measure also marks the beginning of a new, transitional section.

The theme associated with the transition begins in C-sharp

Example 1. *Symphonic Sketches,* mvt. 1, meas. 1–6.

minor (meas. 28). The melody at this point might suggest stylized "Indian music," owing to both its unusual rhythm and its pentatonic melody. Played by the low woodwinds and low strings, it is based on a stack of four perfect fifths, E-B-F sharp-C sharp-G sharp. There is one added note in the theme, D sharp, but it is merely a grace note. The theme is transposed to G-sharp minor in measure 35, where it is played by the first violins, flute, and English horn.

The transition continues in measure 42, sounding the dominant of E major. As the theme begins to fragment, a portion of it is played by the oboes and English horn (meas. 42–43), while the grace note motive (cf. meas. 30–31) follows in the flute and violin parts (meas. 44). At measure 54 the dominant of C major is reached, and the primary melodic material is the grace-note figure.

The secondary section (Part 1/Section 2) begins in C major (meas. 58), where the horns play a pentatonic melody (S^1) that acts as a short introduction to a new theme (Example 2). This brief introductory passage is interesting in itself for Chadwick's employment of horn fifths, one of the composer's favorite techniques. It leads into the new theme (S^2) in the violins in measure 63 (Example 3), a melody that is folksonglike in character, possessing a smooth, arched shape, and a narrow (one-octave) range. One of the most interesting features of this section is its bass line, which adopts the rhythm of a habanera, perhaps a reflection of the influence of Georges Bizet, Louis Moreau Gottschalk, or even ragtime.

Horns

Example 2. *Symphonic Sketches,* mvt. 1, meas. 58–61.

Violin I

Example 3. *Symphonic Sketches,* mvt. 1, meas. 63–67.

In general, the section is very conservative; throughout, the theme is presented primarily by woodwinds and upper strings with frequent doubling by the horns (meas. 64, 72, 79, 88). The section remains steadfastly in C major, the most notable harmonic shift being to the subdominant (meas. 80). After cadencing on the tonic in measure 94, the section swiftly progresses to the development area (meas. 96). Again, the striking habanera rhythm is sounded in the cellos (cf. meas. 64).

The development area begins in measure 96, concentrating on the theme from the preceding section. Most notable is the bass line, which descends by fifths from F to A flat (meas. 96–102). The A flat soon becomes the enharmonic dominant (G-sharp) of the first major section of the development, in C-sharp minor (meas. 110). At measure 110 the principal theme is played in the key of C-sharp minor. It appears transposed to D major in measure 118, and then to E major in 122. In measure 126 an entirely new section is reached, clearly delineated in the score by double bars, and cast in a new meter. After a strongly articulated augmented-sixth chord in measure 144, the development continues in measure 145. Here the grace-note figure associated with the secondary theme is exploited. The motive is played primarily in the woodwinds and strings, and it builds to an explosive climax at the beginning of the recapitulation.

The recapitulation, in two sections, begins in measure 157 in A major. Unlike the first statement of the principal theme, in the opening measures, the statement of the main theme here does not begin with the actual theme, but rather with a thunderous A-major chord, as if Chadwick expected that the main theme was, by now, thoroughly ingrained in the listener's ear, and he needed to provide only the harmonic underpinning. After two measures, the theme emerges, "already in progress," at measure 159. The theme is again heard, transposed to C-sharp minor (meas. 167) and E major (meas. 175). The hemiola passage is revisited (cf. meas. 24) in measure 182 and leads to the next section.

Part 2 of the recapitulation begins in measure 186, where the horn-call theme that introduced the development section is played (cf. meas. 58) in F major. This music is followed by a theme stated earlier (cf. meas. 63), played here by the first violins, and accompanied by the habanera rhythm. At measure 222 the music begins an ascending progression in fourths, beginning on F and moving to B flat (meas. 224), E flat (meas. 226), A flat (meas. 228), and D flat (meas. 230). The D flat progresses to its enharmonic parallel,

C sharp in measure 235. The C sharp then becomes the dominant of F-sharp minor, the key of an earlier transition (cf. meas. 28).

In measure 238 another of Chadwick's multi-sectional codas begins. Its first section relies on thematic material associated with the principal key (cf. meas. 1). It is very fragmented, as if the composer merely wished to hint at his use of the main theme, rather than present it in its entirety. At measure 250, however, A major is reached, and a less fragmented version of the main theme appears for four measures.

The second section of the coda employs the material found in the latter portion of the development section (cf. meas. 126). It is a loud, rhythmic, high-spirited section, the main purpose of which is to provide a stark contrast to the calm of the next section. A fortissimo D-flat major chord (enharmonic to C sharp) brings this section to a close in measure 273.

The coda's third section (meas. 274) is very short; it is eight measures long and brings back a melody first heard in the secondary area (cf. meas. 63). The passage hints at the previous themes in an almost nostalgic manner. This section leads directly into measure 282 and the fourth section.

The fourth section of the coda (meas. 282), also brief, brings back the habanera rhythm, lavishly accompanied by strings, harp, and held notes in the horns and upper woodwinds. The thematic material is also derived from the secondary section (cf. meas. 79–90). At measure 298, the harmonic rhythm of the section slows considerably to provide a contrast with the following section. After a long D pedal (the subdominant of A major) the final section of this movement is reached in measure 315.

Marked "presto," and in A major, the final section is a rousing ending based upon the primary theme. The movement draws to a dramatic close in measure 333.

Movement 2

The second movement of *Symphonic Sketches,* "Noël," is prefaced by the following lines:

Through the soft, calm moonlight comes a sound;
A mother lulls her babe, and all around
The gentle snow lies glistening;
On such a night the Virgin Mother mild
In dreamless slumber wrapped the Holy Child,
While angel-hosts were listening.

The movement is cast in a simple three-part form in D-flat major (see Diagram 4–2).

Diagram 4–2. Formal Structure of "Noël."

		Section 1		
Theme:	Intro.	A		
Key:	$D^{\flat}$:I	I	I	V—I
MM.:	1	5	13	28—29
Comment:	$\frac{3}{4}$	Eng. Hrn.	duet	
		Quasi-Pent.	Ob./E.h.	

								Section 2		
Theme:	t						A	B		
Key:	I	IV	vii^7/V-V			A^6	I	I—V/C:I		
MM.:	29	36	41	42	47-48	49	50	66	81	82
Comment:	frag.				hem.		vln. solo			

			Section 3					
Theme:	A		A					
Key:	ii^{ø7}	Aug^6	I	I				I
MM.:	83—90	91	103	119	125–26	129–30	133	143
Comment:	stretto		inv.		hem.	hem.	vln. solo	

Marked "Andante con tenerezza," the movement begins solemnly with staggered entrances in the strings. After four introductory measures, the main theme is played by the English horn (Example 4). It is characterized by its relatively large range (b flat to d flat^2) and its straightforward descending and ascending line. The structure of the melody is also noteworthy; while it is not

English Horn

Example 4. *Symphonic Sketches,* mvt. 2, meas. 5–8.

pentatonic, it has the pentatonic "feel" that Beveridge refers to in his earlier-mentioned article.[10] Because it emphasizes minor thirds and whole steps, the theme has a sound very similar to that of a strictly pentatonic structure. The English horn is joined by the first oboe (meas. 13), and the duet takes the music to the first cadence in measure 29.

The transition makes use of the material that has already been presented, particularly a three-note cell extracted from the main theme (cf. meas. 6). First heard in the flutes (meas. 29–30), the cell quickly spreads throughout the orchestra. At measure 36 the music pauses at the subdominant before moving on to the climax of the section, on the dominant, at measure 42. The music is punctuated by hemiola in the bass at this point, before progressing into a diminuendo at measure 44. More hemiola appears in the first violins (meas. 47) before the music progresses to an augmented-sixth chord (meas. 49).

Before the section ends there is a final statement of the main theme (meas. 50), still in the key of D flat. The use of the orchestra here differs drastically from its previous presentation; a solo violin plays the theme, and the nature of the accompaniment changes. The harp is introduced for the first time in this movement, while the woodwinds primarily play held notes and the strings play muted pizzicato figures. The orchestration lends the entire section a transparent, somewhat haunting character.

Section 2 of this movement is reached in measure 66. The secondary theme begins in the lower strings, but is quickly joined by the first violins and flute in measure 71 (Example 5). This section is marked by an animated tempo and greater reliance on the woodwinds and brass instruments to strengthen the accompaniment. After the key of C major is reached in measure 82, a stretto section employing the main theme begins in the winds (meas. 83). The winds are underpinned by the upper strings, which play tremolos, sul ponticello in measure 87.

Violin I

Example 5. *Symphonic Sketches,* mvt. 2, meas. 70–73.

The use of the earlier-mentioned rhythmic cell (cf. meas. 6) occurs again in measure 96. It sounds throughout the orchestra until measure 103, where Section 3 begins. The new section presents an inverted, varied version of the main theme in the tonic key, while the brass section plays the primary thematic material. This climactic area displays the virtuosity of Chadwick's orchestration brilliantly; here the composer achieved one of his richest textures by giving the harp chords and employing double stops in the strings. The triplet figures in the bass lend the whole a feeling of rhythmic momentum, while the descending brass and ascending woodwinds and strings (first violins and cellos) present a wonderful clash of instrumental color.

At measure 125, a large section of hemiola begins in the strings and spreads to the winds (meas. 129). The solo violin returns in measure 133, and, after a remnant of the main theme sounds in the clarinet (meas. 137), takes the work to a close in measure 143.

Movement 3

The third movement, subtitled "Hobgoblin," is preceded simply by the following line borrowed from Shakespeare:

> "That shrewd and knavish sprite called Robin Good-fellow"

The music is cast in sonata form in the key of F major (see Diagram 4–3).

Diagram 4–3. Formal Structure of "Hobgoblin."

Theme:	O (Intro.)			
Key:	F:V	V	V	V
MM.:	1	14	26	34
Comment:	Hrn.	Hrn. solo	frag.	

	Part 1 Section 1							
Theme:	P	t	O	P				t
Key:	I	g:V–i		F:I	d:vii^{o7}–i		VI	V–i
MM.:	42	58	66	95	110–11		119	124–5
Comment:				vln.	frag.			frag.

	Section 2			
Theme:	O	t	O	t
Key:	C:I	Aug^6	I	V/d
MM.:	144	164	196	210
Comment:		harp	aug.	A maj.

	Part 2 Section 3				
Theme:	P	(P)	(P)	t	
Key:	d: i	g	c——	g–c–F–B♭–E♭–A♭–C♯/D♭–f♯–B–D♯	
MM.:	222	236	250	258	278
Comment:	Trio bsn.	str.	ob.	frgs.	ped.

						Section 4	
Theme:			O			P	t
Key:			F: V		V	I	g:i
MM.:	282	290	298	315	316–17	318	334
Comment:	mixed meter	harp		ferm.			

					Coda 1	Coda 2	
Theme:	O		t	O/P	O		
Key:	V				F:I	V–I——	I
MM.:	371	387–90	391	405–6	423	479	500
Comment:		hem.			brass	hem.	

Subtitled “Scherzo capriccioso,” the movement begins with a long introduction. A vibrant horn call sounds in measure 1. Here, as in the Second Symphony, Chadwick demonstrated his delight in employing the horn for an introductory solo passage (cf. Symphony No. 2, mvt. 1, meas. 1). After the horn call the strings and woodwinds enter (meas. 6), followed by another statement of the horn call, transposed down an octave, in measure 14. At measure 26 the music reaches the dominant; it proceeds to measure 42, where the main theme is introduced.

The main theme (Example 6), first heard in the clarinets, is a sprightly invention that eventually lends itself to a great deal of development. The consequent phrase, which leads to G minor, begins in measure 51. A transition then begins. Fragments of the in-

Example 6. *Symphonic Sketches,* mvt. 3, meas. 42–49.

troductory horn call are played by the cellos in measure 66, after which main theme fragments are sounded throughout the orchestra (meas. 69). In measure 75, the woodwinds introduce an eighth-note passage that the strings take up in measure 81. The strings lead to a section of hemiola on the dominant (meas. 93). A second statement of the main theme begins in measure 95, again on the tonic. The music begins to fragment in measure 110, where the key of D minor is reached. By measure 119 the music is in the key of B-flat major, and the main theme is heard above hemiola in the accompanying strings. The first section draws to a close after fragments of the main theme are heard (meas. 127 to 141). After the presentation of a cadential ritardando (via hemiola) is sounded in the woodwinds (meas. 142–3), Section 2 begins in measure 144.

The theme associated with the secondary key is based on the opening horn call (cf. meas. 1). It is played by the violins in their low register and by the violas (Example 7). The theme evokes a Celtic jig or a similar dance, and the numerous grace notes add to that impression. At measure 160 the entire orchestra begins a hemiola passage that lasts until measure 164, where a transitional section begins. The transition starts with an augmented-sixth chord. The remainder of the section, characterized by tremolos in the winds and strings, occasional staccato figures, and arpeggios in the harp, is an excellent example of Chadwick's interest in effects that evoke the mystical or oriental.

Although he had often used pentatonicism, a technique that is also part of the language of impressionism, here is the composer's

Example 7. *Symphonic Sketches,* mvt. 3, meas. 142–50.

first venture in his symphonic works into other aspects of that language. The diminished sonorities and absence of thematic material also add to this effect. At measure 178 the music introduces fragments of both the main theme, in the strings, and the secondary theme, in the woodwinds. These crescendo, after a hemiola in measure 190, into an augmented version of the secondary theme played by the brass section "tutta forza." In measure 210 the key of A major is reached, the dominant of D minor, the key in which the next section opens.

The development section begins in measure 222 with hemiola in the strings and a theme played by the bassoons, which is actually a hybrid of the two preceding themes (Example 8). Measures 222–223 are closely related to the material found in measure 42, while measures 226–228 resemble the opening horn call. This theme represents a clever melding of two ideas that have been heard from the inception of the movement, but the relationships are easily overlooked because of the humorous and interesting accompaniment, which consists of dialogue and hocketlike exchanges among the string instruments and tremolos in the woodwinds. The theme is continued in the strings (meas. 236) in the key of G minor. A fragment of it is heard in the oboes in measure 250, before the music reaches a transition in measure 258.

The transition section is most notable for its harmonic progression down the circle of fifths; the music begins in G minor (meas. 258), and progresses to C minor (meas. 260), F major (meas. 262), B-flat major (meas. 264), E-flat major (meas. 266), A-flat major (meas. 268), and D-flat/C-sharp major (meas. 270), F-sharp minor (meas. 272), B major (meas. 274). A D-sharp pedal is reached in measure 278, while fragments of the main theme are played by the strings and woodwinds. In measure 282 the meter changes to $\frac{4}{4}$ in the clarinet part, while the rest of the orchestra remains in $\frac{3}{4}$. While the line remains in $\frac{4}{4}$ meter for only four measures, the juxtaposition of duple and triple serves to create a sense of confusion before reaching measure 290. Here the harp engages in a dialogue with staccato figures in the violins to the accompaniment of held

Example 8. *Symphonic Sketches,* mvt. 3, meas. 222–228.

notes and pizzicato lower strings. The horn call from the introduction reappears in measure 298. As in the beginning of the movement, the horn call is introductory to the principal theme, which, at this point, marks the recapitulation.

The recapitulation begins in measure 318, where the main theme is once again sounded in the tonic. After the theme is heard in the flute in measure 333, it is developed as it was in the exposition. The eighth-note figures encountered earlier (meas. 75) reappear and lead to a hemiola, sounded throughout the orchestra, in measure 369. At measure 371 the secondary theme is played by the horns in the dominant, leading to a transition in measure 391. The harp appears once again, and a mystical/oriental section begins in measure 393 (cf. meas. 164 and 290). Fragments of the main theme and the secondary theme begin in measure 405, displaying a type of juxtaposition the composer favored (cf. this movement, meas. 222–232). This leads directly to the coda, which begins in measure 423.

The coda is in two parts. The first, marked "Animato assai," reiterates the brass chorale version of the horn theme played earlier by the brass section (cf. meas. 196). A fortissimo ninth chord is sounded in measure 445, marking one of the most harmonically daring moments in this movement. The rest of this part of the coda is devoted to progressing to the next section that begins in measure 479. The second part of the coda, marked "assai con fuoco," begins with eight measures of hemiola, leading to a grand pause in measure 488. After a second grand pause in measure 490, the movement moves briskly to a close in measure 500.

Movement 4

The fourth movement of the *Symphonic Sketches,* subtitled "A Vagrom Ballad," is prefaced by these lines:

A tale of tramps and railway ties,
Of old clay pipes and rum,
Of broken heads and blackened eyes
And the "thirty days" to come!

This work constitutes one of the composer's most entertaining and effective efforts. The movement is a five-part structure in the key of A minor, and is marked "Moderato. Alla Burla" (see Diagram 4–4).

Diagram 4–4. Formal Structure of "A Vagrom Ballad."

				Part 1			
Theme:	Intro.	Cad.		P			
Key:	a:V^7		V^6_5	i		C:V–I	I
MM.:	1	9–10	14	16	22	23	29
Comment:		bs.cl.		bsns. bs.cl.	sync. rhythm		

						Part 2		
Theme:	t^1				t^2	P		t^2
Key:		B♭—B♭		a:V	i———d:V	i		B♭
MM.:	30	32	36	38	39	55	71	73
Comment:	d^7ths	trpt. fanfare	ferm.		a ped.		xyl.	cad.

		Part 3				
Theme:		P			(P)	(P)
Key:		g:V–i		A♭:V–I	D♭:I	F
MM.:	75	87	95	101	103	106
Comment:	d ped.	hrns.	brass perc.		frag.	

		Part 4		
Theme:	t^2	(t^2)	(P)	
Key:	F	a: $vii^{ø7}$/V	————	V
MM.:	125	146	152	156
Comment:	sync.		brass soli	

Theme:	P	t^2					
Key:	a:i		F:V^7	I	V	I	B♭
MM.:	170	176	181	182	191	193	197——201
Comment:	str.		sync.		xyl.		trpt. ferm.

	Part 5		
Theme:	N		
Key:	A: V^7/V	I^6_4	V
MM.:	202	222	243–44
Comment:	Lento	E ped.	cad. bs.cl.

	Coda 1				Coda 2	
Theme:						
Key:	A:I	I	V	V	I	I
MM.:	245	265	273	280	281	301
Comment:	$\frac{6}{8}$	$\frac{2}{4}$	E ped.	ferm.	Prest.	

The movement begins softly with bassoons, which are soon joined by the strings and remaining woodwind instruments. Fermatas in measures 9 and 10 allow an ad lib. solo by the bass clarinet. Chadwick's choice of this unusual instrument, sometimes comical sounding and often a bit clumsy is witness to the fact that he was wryly taking his "Alla burla" instruction to heart. It is also apparent that the composer found the greatest humor in the lower instruments. Several measures of transition take the music to a fermata in measure 15, after which the first section begins.

Part 1 begins in measure 16 with its theme, in A minor, played by the bass clarinet and bassoons (Example 9).

This is perhaps the composer's most humorous melody; the strumming figures in the violins recall the banjo, and the sometimes "ragged" rhythms of the melody (meas. 22), possibly based on ragtime, make it unique among Chadwick's work. The key of C major is reached in measure 23, followed by the key of B flat and the appearance of a military-style fanfare in the muted trumpets and the snare drum. This section leads to another fermata in measure 36 and on to a brief transition beginning in measure 39. The transition is very rhythmic, drawing upon the earlier theme (cf. meas. 16). The first part closes in measure 54 on the dominant of D minor.

Part 2 introduces a variation of the main theme, played by the clarinets and violas. There is only a slight alteration from the statements of this theme heard in Part 1. The greatest changes actually occur in the accompaniment, which is generally more active than in the earlier passages. Throughout this section the woodwinds and brass interact more with the melody, and gaps between fragments of the melody have been elongated to provide more space for dialogue between melody and accompaniment (as, for example,

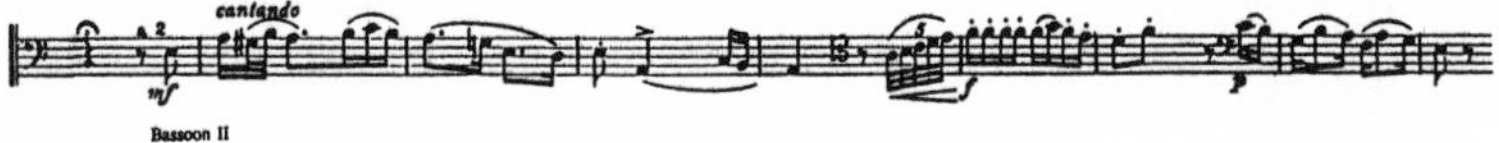

Example 9. *Symphonic Sketches,* mvt. 4, meas. 16–23.

in meas. 60–61). The melody soon becomes fragmented, and in measures 66–67 a part of the melody is clearly played by the strings (cf. meas. 25–26). The xylophone appears in measure 71 and takes the music to B-flat major at the "animato" in measure 73 (cf. meas. 39). A D pedal leads to G minor for the next section.

Part 3 begins in G minor with a melody that is yet another derivative of the main theme. Played by the horns, it clearly reflects the influence of Dvořák (Example 10). The orchestration, again highlighted by Chadwick's preference for the horn (see Symphony No. 2, op. 21, mvt. 1, meas. 1), features swirling inner strings, lightly scored winds, and a running bass line. The melody is quasi-pentatonic; the only pitch present that is not in the D - F - G - B flat - C pentatonic structure is A. As has been noted earlier, however, an additional tone, when used in certain ways, will sound as though it belongs to the pentatonic scale. In this case, the A appears only as a neighboring tone or a passing tone.

The melody is repeated by the trumpets and trombones in measure 95, where the percussion section (including snare drum, bass drum, and cymbals) enters. A false entrance of the theme is played (meas. 104) before the theme itself is presented in F major (meas. 106). Beginning at measure 109 the music progresses through a developmental section that features primarily B-flat minor. The rhythm begins to slow in measure 114, and accents change from one measure to the next. At measure 119 the strings play in triple meter against the rest of the orchestra, again upsetting the rhythmic stability of the texture. At measure 125, a transition begins, based on material previously sounded (cf. meas. 39 and 73).

Section 4 begins in A minor at measure 146, with the sounding of a half-diminished seventh chord built on D sharp. The thematic material is that used for the transitional section just stated (cf. meas. 125). This is the most developmental section of the movement, relying upon thematic fragmentation and rapid changes of harmony throughout. The dominant of A minor sounds in measure

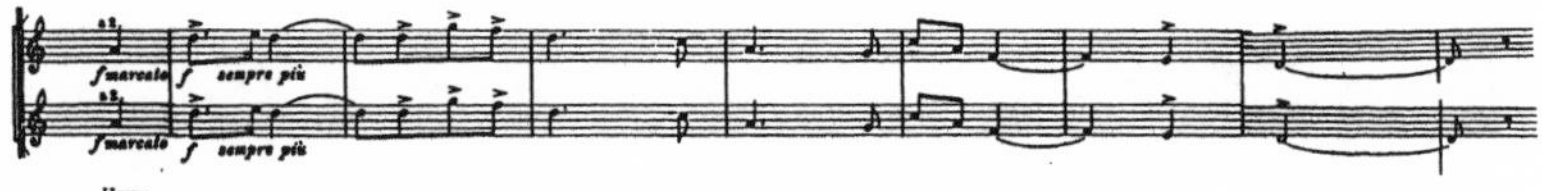

Example 10. *Symphonic Sketches,* mvt. 4, meas. 87–94.

156 and takes the music to measure 166, where a chromatic descent begins in the bass line. The descent leads to the dominant of A minor in measure 169 and thence to measure 170, where the theme from Part 3 is sounded (cf. meas. 87), this time by the trumpets and violins. The statement is interrupted by a fragment of the transitional theme (cf. meas. 125) in measures 176–177. The main theme continues until measure 191, where the xylophone enters again, now on the dominant. The tonic is reached in measure 193 and the subdominant in measure 197. Here the fanfare theme returns (cf. meas. 32) before the fermata occurs in measure 201.

Section 5 is one of the composer's most curious inventions. Marked "Lento misterioso," the music is an impressionistic parody of the style of Debussy (Example 11).

Chadwick could not have had many opportunities to hear Debussy's music performed by an orchestra; the French master's works were not performed by the Boston Symphony Orchestra until well into the twentieth century, and even then they were not performed with any regularity. Yet, this section features many of the traits that one might find in much of Debussy's music, the *Prelude a l'apres-midi d'un faune,* for example, including lean

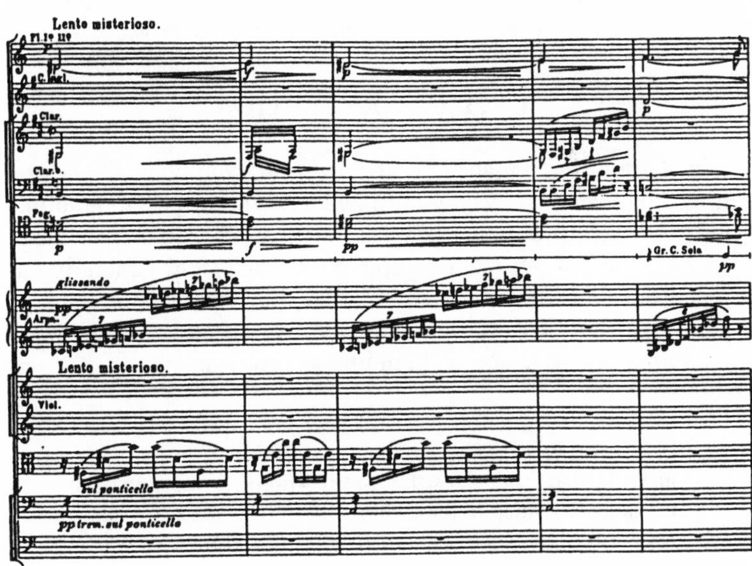

Example 11. *Symphonic Sketches,* mvt. 4, meas. 202–206.

orchestration, nonfunctional harmony, and special effects such as harp glissandi, static woodwind parts, tremolos, and sul ponticello markings in the strings. It is certainly doubtful that Chadwick learned the style and techniques of impressionism independently. As a knowledgeable musician and pedagogue who kept a careful eye on trends in composition, he was certainly aware of the latest French contributions even if only from his study of the scores.

In measure 207 the strings begin a recitativelike statement that dominates the rest of the section. A descending bass line (meas. 218) leads to A major in measure 222, and the strings continue their statement to the accompaniment of held notes and glissandi. The section progresses to the dominant of A (meas. 243), where the bass clarinet presents another cadenza, this time a bit longer, which brings the section to a close.

The coda, entirely in A major, is in two sections. The first is marked "Molto vivace" in $\frac{6}{8}$ meter. The music at this point bears strikingly little resemblance to any of the music heard earlier in the movement, unlike Chadwick's normal practice. The dominant is reached in measure 280 and takes the music to the second part of the coda in measure 281. Marked "Prestissimo" and using previously employed material (cf. meas. 222), it is a rousing, fortissimo passage in finale style that ends in measure 301.

CRITICAL RECEPTION

In a 1904 performance by the Boston Symphony Orchestra, three movements of *Symphonic Sketches,* "Jubilee," "Hobgoblin," and "A Vagrom Ballad," were performed. The slow movement, "Noël," had not yet been completed. Critics were generally enthusiastic about the three works that they heard, although the anonymous music critic of the *Boston Herald* reviewed the work in a rather dry style and without undue verbiage:

> "Hobgoblin," after one hearing, does not appear to be so individual a work as its companions, "Jubilee" and "A Vagrom Ballad," nor does the music wholly fit the title. The music is too much in the clear sunlight; it is not sufficiently mysterious, uncanny spectral. "A Vagrom Ballad" was performed here last season at a Chickering concert, and the strong impression then made by it was confirmed. It is a bal-

> lad that might be hoarsely sung by tramp or pirate, or by any one that has freed himself from the shackles of respectability. It is the apotheosis of the open road, or of the cutlass, plank and jolly Roger.[11]

It is worth noting that the reviewer failed to pen his thoughts about "Jubilee," a movement that has traditionally been a favorite among audiences and critics. The critic is, of course, correct in his assertion that "Hobgoblin" is not as individual as the other two movements.

Another reviewer wrote ebulliently of the performance, expressing his admiration for "Vagrom Ballad" above the other movements and comparing Chadwick to the "modern" school of composers:

> This was one of the set of Symphonic sketches [*sic*] in which Mr. Chadwick showed that he could be as modern as any Straussite or Wagnerian of them all. Modern orchestral coloring, freedom of form and treatment, bold and fiery mood-painting was in every measure of this striking work.[12]

Chadwick's orchestration and ingenious use of instruments delighted this reviewer more than other aspects of the work. He went on to describe the impressions made by the music and peppered them with the hope that perhaps other great orchestras around the nation would program the composition:

> At the very beginning of the work the bassoon, used prominently in the score, gave a note of grotesqueness and sardonic power that was sustained throughout, and the bass-clarinette [*sic*] had some very impressive touches near the end. The contrasts were made with enormous effect. We earnestly hope that Thomas, in Chicago, Paur, in Pittsburgh, and Gericke, in Boston, will give this number a hearing in the symphony concerts of their respective cities. It is as bold a "Humoreske" as any in the American repertoire and ought to become standard.[13]

The writer ended with several more accolades for Chadwick's accomplishments before closing with an insightful statement about Chadwick, Dvořák, and American folk music:

> The ability of this composer in the line of Scherzo was again illustrated both by the "Jubilee" and the "Hobgoblin." The first-named leans toward the music of the plantation, and causes us to state again that Mr. Chadwick used this American folk-music (in his second symphony) long before Dvorak [*sic*] wrote his "From the New World" [*sic*] symphony, on plantation themes.[14]

Symphonic Sketches was first performed as a complete, four-movement work on February 7, 1908, by the Boston Symphony Orchestra. The reviews were unprecedentedly favorable in the history of Chadwick's symphonies. One critic, echoing the column cited above, wrote:

> Mr. Chadwick was the first to sound a distinctly American note in good orchestral music. Long before Dvorak [*sic*] advised the classical employment of the American folk-song, Mr. Chadwick had used it in the scherzo of his second symphony, suggesting the southern plantation.[15]

The writer continued enthusiastically, comparing Chadwick's compositions to well-known European works; "Hobgoblin," he stated, was the "American Queen Mab," "Vagrom Ballad" the "American Till Eulenspiegel," and "Jubilee" reminded him of a circus band.[16]

In one of the longest and most perceptive reviews that Chadwick ever received, the well-known critic Henry T. Parker discussed the composer's contribution to music, frequently comparing him with other well-known American musicians:

> Mr. Chadwick, as his "Symphonic Sketches" suggested once more at the Symphony Concert of Saturday, is the most American of our composers, because oftener than with the rest his music in mood and in spirit sounds distinctively American. For a composer to live permanently and work steadily in America is not to write American music. Mr. Loeffler, for example, so lives and works, but there is not an American trait so far as we can recall in his music. To have been born in America is no title to the writing of American music as the compositions of Templeton Strong, Arthur Bird and sundry other Teutonized Americans readily proves. In fact and in suggestion it is "made in Germany" as truly as

> though it were so invoiced in some musical customhouse. To write music from the melodies of primitive peoples, like the Indians or the Negroes, who happen to live on American soil, is to write music that is only geographically American. Dvorak [*sic*] was still a Czech when he wrote such a symphony and called it "From the New World"; Mr. Farwell and all his brethren are often only experimenting with an aboriginal music that has nothing to do with the American spirit of today. Mr. MacDowell was narrowly individual through and through, and he would have dreamed his dreams of Arthur's court, Celtic queens and Norse warriors anywhere, and shaped his "Woodland Sketches" or his sea-pieces as readily in Wiesbaden as in Boston.[17]

Parker went on to discuss other national styles, noting that what is distinct about them is not their use of folk songs, but rather the spirit with which they are imbued:

> And so forth and so on with other American composers. Russian music, with all allowance for its folk-tunes and its other palpable Russian idiosyncrasies, is Russian because the mood and the spirit of it is clearly recognizable as such. The mood and spirit of Sibelius's symphonies and tone-poems, again, is unmistakably of the North. Smetana's music is Bohemian, not because Bohemian legends stirred his fancy or he utilized Bohemian tunes, but because in temper and atmosphere [it] is clearly Czech. Massenet's smack of Paris even when he imagines he is more German than Wagner or more Italian than Mascagni. Cho-Cho-San [*sic*] is a geisha of Japan, but her voice in Puccini's "Madame Butterfly" is Italianate with her passion. A score of other examples are as ready, to prove that the true test of nationality in music is not any comparatively extraneous circumstances, but its underlying, pervading and persuading spirit.[18]

The critic then explained that Chadwick, like the many fine composers mentioned above, was able to capture the essence of his own national experience. Parker continued:

> Mr. Chadwick's music seems so often American because it bears this test. Recall, for example, the scherzo of one of his symphonies–that in F, if we remember rightly–and its mood is altogether American. Black, "buck" roustabouts dance on

> the wharf; an American composer watches them and puts into his music their soul and his. Recall the "Columbian Ode" for the World's Fair at Chicago—American in each succeeding mood of pride in the past, exultation in the present, and confidence in the future. Recall a movement here and there in Mr. Chadwick's chamber music, and again comes memory of a distinctly American spirit.[19]

Finally, Parker discussed Chadwick's music and the Boston Symphony Orchestra's performance:

> Turn, in particular, to the "Symphonic Sketches," as Dr. Muck and his men played them on Friday and Saturday. He is German; they are of many nationalities, and, being foreigners, he and they perhaps sentimentalized the slow, contrasting passages of the first and last "sketches" more than a sensitive American conductor and band would do. Allow for this; and grant, too, that the nocturne of parental affection and longing of the second "sketch" is universal and not particular in spirit. The three other "sketches" remain and in them the mood is vividly, stirringly, and, in two at least, irresistibly American. Americans "fool," Americans "jolly," and European observers are fain to lament these ingrained habits in us. Is Mr. Chadwick's final "sketch"—"The Vagrom Ballad" of "clay pipes and rum and broken heads and blackened eyes and thirty days to come"—anything else than musical "fooling" and musical "jollying," American in spirit and expression, and often at its loudest and most careless? Comes the slow, mysterious, sober song near the end. The inevitable "contrasting passage," the merely academic may call it. As it seems to us, it is far more a just musical incarnation of the tendency in the American temperament to turn suddenly serious, and deeply and unaffectedly so, in the midst of its "fooling," to run away into sober fancies and moods, and then as quickly turn "jolly" again.[20]

Unlike many other critics, Parker noted that Chadwick's melodies were not the only element of his craft to contribute to the feeling of "American-ness." The sudden shifts of mood also contributed significantly to the style. Much of Parker's analysis, however, deals not with Chadwick's employment of technique, but with the composer's innate sense of what it is to be a Yankee. Parker continued,

> Return through the scherzo of "Hobgoblin," and it is bluff music with an unmistakable sturdy American tang. Mr. Chadwick has taken his boy-fairy out of the English farmsteads to set him in American farm houses. He is a Hobgoblin who musically sets his ten fingers to his nose like the American hobbledehoy that he is. Pass to the first "sketch" of "Jubilee." Here, as now and then elsewhere in Mr. Chadwick's later music, is the echo of Negro tunes; but the American quality of the music lies little in that. Rather it is in the high and volatile spirits of the music, the sheer rough-and-tumble of it at its fullest moments. As was said on Saturday, the music shouts because it cannot help it, and it sings because it cannot help it, and each as only an American would shout and sing. And the intervening suaver passage, as in the last movement, is only the other face of this American volatility.[21]

Finally, Parker concluded his substantial review by defining the essence of American music. The debate that rages among scholars still, concerning the definition and the nature of American music, is responded to directly and without hesitation:

> No, Mr. Chadwick does not write American music because he was born in Lowell or because he lives and works in Boston, or because he now and then recalls an American folk-tune. He writes it because it is often, and especially of late years, intrinsically, American in mood, spirit, and appeal.[22]

The music reviewer for the *Boston Globe* attended the 1908 concert, and, although he was pleased with what he heard, the tone of the article is less enthusiastic than was Parker's. After noting that each movement of *Symphonic Sketches* is prefaced by verse, the writer continued,

> In every instance Prof. Chadwick has developed his ideas skilfully, and although utilizing modern methods and expressing the motifs by a modern orchestra, he is lucid and melodic in his forms, and his music is good to hear, for it is music that the average ear finds pleasing.
>
> Skilled in scoring for orchestras and naturally a musician of original ideas, he has composed four little works that are valuable additions to musical literature. There is a deal of the

> "American" in the "Jubilee" part, with its strong rhythms and tunes. The theme upon which "Noël" is based is plaintive in character, effective and very cleverly worked out.
>
> In the "Hobgoblin" section the composer fairly reveled in quaint, intermittent and oddly accentuated bits of orchestration, suggesting Strauss at times, yet keeping well within bounds and avoiding too much of the discordant. And in this will-o-the-wisp music the orchestra appeared as effective as in the gentler and more connected score of the previous number [Noël].
>
> The moanings of the clarinet and xylophone and the contrasts in a tramp's life on the road as set to music in "A Vagrom Ballad" were very amusing, the story being told in musical pictures that vividly exemplified that text. The suite is so thoroughly enjoyable that it should become one of the lighter "stand-bys" of the orchestra. The audience expressed great delight at the spirited performance of this admirable work.[23]

Chadwick should have been pleased with the reviews that he received for the 1908 performance of *Symphonic Sketches*. Without exception, critics responded favorably to his unique style. Although the work contained some minor flaws, the general reaction by critics and audiences placed the composition and the composer firmly among the ranks of the great American composers.

Symphonic Sketches was revived by the Boston Symphony Orchestra in 1918. Philip Hale, the great critic who had reviewed Chadwick's Third Symphony many years before, was present at the performance. His thoughts on the music were extremely positive, perhaps not only as tribute to the music, but to the composer who had in the intervening years become a formidable figure on the American music scene. Hale's review looks backward to a time when critics had written that the composition embodied the spirit of its time and place. He wrote:

> Mr. Chadwick's Sketches, especially "Jubilee" and "A Vagrom Ballad," may justly be called American music. Not because the two are derived in any way from Congo, Indian, Creole or Cowboy themes; not because they strive to illustrate in tones an episode in American history or to portray some prominent American; but because this music has characteristics, rhythmic [and] melodic that we believe to be distinctively American; because it is vitalized by a peculiarly

> American spirit. The middle Sketches, "Noel [*sic*] and "Hobgoblin," pleasing as they are, might have been composed by a musician of another nationality. It is impossible to think of anyone but an American inventing the material of the other two and evolving the expression, the musical speech for the thought.[24]

Hale went on to point out exactly what he believed caused Chadwick's music to be particularly American:

> There is an originality, a swing, an audacity, a recklessness, an irreverence—witness the introduction of a phrase from Bach's great organ fugue in G minor in "A Vagrom Ballad"; a joyous extravagance, a rollicking humor, a boastfulness tempered slightly by appreciation of the ridiculous; an utter absence of self-consciousness, and inability to take oneself or one's achievements too seriously—all phases of the American character that we find in Walt Whitman's "Leaves of Grass"; in the stories of "O. Henry"; even in certain pages of Thoreau and Emerson. "Jubilee" and "A Vagrom Ballad" might also be called "human documents."[25]

Chadwick's *Symphonic Sketches* was not of interest solely for its "American-ness," however. By 1918, many American concertgoers were hoping that at a given concert they might be treated to something positive, something life-affirming. Hale summed up these feelings when he wrote:

> In these days when young composers are gloomy, pessimistic in music, when they strive to translate a tragedy into tones, to express the Infinite in a symphonic poem, it is a good thing to be reminded that music may be gay, exhilarating, and thus beneficent, and at the same time show the hand of the skilled musician.[26]

Hale completed his heartfelt review by commenting on the performance:

> The Sketches were brilliantly played and heartily enjoyed by the large audience. Dr. Muck conducted them con amore. Mr. Chadwick was obliged to acknowledge the spontaneous and prolonged applause.[27]

CHAPTER 8

SINFONIETTA IN D MAJOR

HISTORY

In his second quasi-symphony, *Sinfonietta,* Chadwick reverted to the more serious and austere style of composing found in his first three symphonies. Although the *Sinfonietta* exhibits many trademarks of his later style, including techniques employed in *Symphonic Sketches,* the work is less programmatic than its predecessor and does not display Chadwick's humorous side with the same vigor. The reason for Chadwick's change of style in the present work cannot be discerned with any certainty; perhaps the critical success that he achieved with *Symphonic Sketches* gave him hope for a similar reception in a more serious work.

In general, Chadwick adhered in the *Sinfonietta* to a traditional symphonic scheme: a first movement sonata form, followed by a ternary allegretto movement, a third movement scherzo, and a finale, also in sonata form.

The *Sinfonietta* relies on smaller orchestral forces than Chadwick had employed in *Symphonic Sketches,* and this lends the work a delicacy and charm that is lacking in the earlier work. The size of each orchestral group has been reduced to include three flutes (one doubling piccolo), paired oboes, clarinets, and bassoons, four horns, two trumpets, three trombones, timpani, snare drum, bass drum, triangle, cymbals, harp, and strings.

The work was composed in 1904 and was premiered in Boston in the same year with the composer conducting. It is the only one of Chadwick's six symphonic works that does not bear a dedication.

ANALYSIS

Movement 1

The first movement of the *Sinfonietta* employs sonata form (see Diagram 5–1).

Diagram 5–1. Formal Structure of First Movement.

		Part 1 Section 1									
Theme:	Intro.	P									
Key:	D:I	I	I^6	V	V	F:I	F	B^b	E^b	A^b	D^b
MM.:	1–4	5	17	21	29	30	34	36	37	39	40
Comment:						hrn.					

		Section 2							
Theme:	t	S					(S)	k	
Key:	G	$f^{\#}$:i	V/III	III	V/III	i	$F^{\#}$:I	V-I	II
MM.:	44	54	71	72	74	81	83	92	106
Comment:									

					Part 2 Section 3					
Theme:			(P)		P					
Key:	D:V/V	V	I	V	I^7	V	V	V	A^b:V	I
MM.:	113	114	116	124	128	132	138	145		149–50
Comment:										

Theme:		(P)						
Key:	g:vii^{o7}	iv^7	i	d:V^6_5	i	B^b:I-V-I	A^b:V-I	b:V/V
MM.:	152	156–57		161–62		169 173	176–77	179
Comment:								

					Section 4					
Theme:	t				S					
Key:	V	II	B^b	b:$ii^{\o 6}_5$	i	i	D:I	V^7	B:V^7	I
MM.:	180	184	189	193	194	204	212	214		220–21
Comment:										

									Coda		
Theme:	(S)		k		(S)		(P)		S	(S)	(P)
Key:	I	V^7	I	G:V	I	V	C:V^7		F#:I	d:i	VI
MM.:	223	231–32		254	256	264	268		278	286	292
Comment:											

Theme:						
Key:	Aug^6	i	iv	D:V^7	I	I
MM.:	294	295	296	299	300	318
Comment:			hrns.		hem.	

Marked "Risolutamente," it begins with three introductory measures that clearly establish its $\frac{3}{4}$ meter and its key. The theme associated with the principal key appears in measure 5 in the violins (Example 1). The melody embodies characteristics of a folk song at first (meas. 5–6), but its large range (b to f-sharp ^{3}) and its quickness are not vocal in style. The rhythmic vitality of the theme, its changing accentuation, and its diversity make it highly suitable for "classical" symphonic development. The passage shifts to the neighborhood of the parallel minor of the dominant in measures 12–16, where the theme is first played by the lower woodwinds and then picked up by the flutes, clarinets, and bassoons. They are joined by the oboes in measure 17, where the music returns to D major. Development of the introductory material (cf. meas. 1–3) begins as early as measure 21, where the string section sounds the dominant. A horn solo occurs in measure 30, and its material is soon transferred to the clarinet (meas. 31) and flute (meas. 33). The violins enter with the theme in E-flat major (meas. 37). D flat is reached unexpectedly in measure 40. Fragments of the main theme are played in measure 44, and a chromatically descending bass (D to BB) leads to employment of the Phrygian mode, built on F sharp, in measure 54. The use of the Phrygian mode marks Chadwick's first experiment in his symphonies with modal language, and, as with his use of orientalisms and employment of the techniques of impressionism in the earlier

Example 1. *Sinfonietta,* mvt. 1, meas. 5–13.

Symphonic Sketches, further reflects his ongoing concern for creating new and interesting sounds. Chadwick was no doubt familiar with Brahms's use of the Phrygian mode in his Third Symphony, but it seems probable that Chadwick's use of the mode stems more from his familiarity with its use by French composers, for Brahms used modality only infrequently, and at the time of the composition of the present work the latest French techniques were very much in vogue. Another important moment in the transition is the change of meter to $\frac{2}{4}$ in the first violins and clarinets in measures 49–53. The sudden change of rhythm, which creates a sense of rhythmic imbalance, makes for a striking and unusual shift leading into the next section.

The secondary theme is played by solo flute and bassoon with contrapuntal imitation in the clarinets in measure 54 (Example 2). This melody has an oriental character that results from its general shape as well as from the instrumentation that Chadwick employed here. The swirling melody, accompanied by the soft, staccato strings, and especially the combination of the harp and triangle, all add to the "chinoise" effect. It is somewhat surprising to find these effects in Chadwick's music; the cult of orientalism did not achieve a widespread following in the United States until a few years later, when its greatest American exponent, Charles Tomlinson Griffes (1884–1920) became interested in the Far East and gave it its most characteristic expression in his tone poem *The Pleasure-Dome of Kubla Khan* (1912). As was pointed out earlier, however, Chadwick was keenly aware of the music of Debussy and others of the French modernist school. The fact that he incorporated the latest trends into his own highly personal style evidences Chadwick's open-mindedness in matters of composition.

The section continues to measure 83 where the clarinets and flutes continue the presentation of the secondary theme in parallel thirds. A closing area, marked "Con moto," begins in measure 92. It features a new melody in the low register of the violins, accompanied by the string section and lightly scored winds. While

Example 2. *Sinfonietta,* mvt. 1, meas. 54–62.

the orchestration at this point is sparse, the closed position of the harmonies gives richness to the sonority and a dense texture. At measure 114, where the dominant of D major leads to a tonic chord in measure 116, fragments of the main theme reappear.

The development section begins in measure 128, where the main theme begins above a dominant seventh chord built on D. The melody is played by the strings and some woodwinds, while the remaining winds and timpani accompany. There is less thematic manipulation than one might expect in the development; the section explores tonalities instead, at least until measure 156. The music moves through several keys and does not show any evidence of following a systematic scheme. Beginning in measure 128 in D, the music moves through A-flat major (meas. 150), G minor (meas. 157), D minor (meas. 162), B-flat major (meas. 169), and A-flat major (meas. 177), before reaching the retransition passage at measure 180.

The most interesting and perhaps most important feature of the development is the fugato section that begins in measure 156. While the counterpoint does not last long (the actual imitative part extends only to measure 174) and it is certainly not Chadwick's most inventive fugato, it was his first such passage since the Third Symphony. Clearly the *Sinfonietta* returns to an older style of composition, one that Chadwick had taken leave of when he composed his *Symphonic Sketches*.

The recapitulation is reached in measure 194 but does not begin in the expected way. The section begins in the key of B minor, rather than in the tonic D. Furthermore, the theme that is recapitulated is that associated with the secondary key (cf. meas. 54). It is important to note that the original statement of the secondary theme was in F-sharp minor, a fourth below the present B minor statement, thus establishing the dominant-tonic relationship. Further, the recapitulation adopts a developmental manner; from this point until the end there are only fragmentary presentations of the principal theme. The composer chose instead to exploit the secondary theme, as well as the closing theme (cf. meas. 92), which appears in measure 232. Similarly, the principal key does not appear until well into the coda. The drama of the development thus continues into this section, with the recapitulation constantly modulating. It begins in B minor (meas. 194) and progresses through D major (meas. 212), B major (meas. 221), and G major (meas. 256).

The coda begins at measure 278 in F-sharp major and progresses to D minor in measure 292, where the violins play a fragment of the principal theme. The tonic D major is not reached until measure 300, where several measures of hemiola and post-cadential harmonic coloring are sounded by the brass section. After a brief, unexpected progression through the minor subdominant and a penultimate C-major chord (meas. 312–313), each of which lends the section a somewhat modal flavor, the movement ends in measure 318 in the tonic.

Movement 2

The second movement of the *Sinfonietta,* entitled "Canzonetta" and marked "Allegretto," is reminiscent of the marchlike dance called the farandole. This dance type was utilized by many composers, particularly French ones. Chadwick's employment of this dance type here seems most closely related to the farandole movement of Bizet's *L'Arlesienne*. The scoring and melodic shape of the two are similar, and it is very likely that Chadwick knew the work well. The American composer had ample opportunity to hear the work, as it was performed by the Boston Symphony Orchestra at least four times between 1893 and 1902.[1]

The first movement is cast in a simple three-part form and begins in A minor without an introduction (see Diagram 5–2).

Diagram 5–2. Formal Structure of Second Movement.

Section 1

Theme:	P			P	t				
Key:	a:i	V	V	i	N^6	i^6	i		i
MM.:	1	8	16	24	30	38	41	42	50
Comment:	stacc.		leg.					vla. solo	

Section 2

Theme:	P^1				t				P^1	
Key:	A:I	V	V/vi	vi	V^7/D	$^{\flat}$III	V$^6_4$	V	I	D:V-I
MM.:	51	59	65	66	67	71	75	79	83	96–97
Comment:										

Section 3

Theme:		P				t			
Key:	D-C-B-B	a:i	V^6	V	i	N^6	V^6	i^6	V
MM.:	99	104	111	119	127	134	137	141	143
Comment:	descent								

Theme:							P^1	
Key:	i	i	i	iv	VI	IV	I	I
MM.:	144	145	153	154	155	156	157	162
Comment:							horn solo	fermata

The principal theme is played by the first violins (Example 3) and accompanied by the remainder of the string section. The melody is one of Chadwick's most unassuming themes, a soft, sempre staccato melody that gives the impression of sounding from afar. In measure 16 the strings cadence on the dominant, where the winds enter as if to answer the preceding string passage. The style of the music at this point changes from the clearly articulated opening few measures to smooth, legato phrasing. The oboe and clarinet present the opening melody in measure 24 to the accompaniment of the strings and take the music to the transition, which begins in measure 30.

The transition begins on the Neapolitan sixth chord with a descending progression in the basses from d to C (meas. 30–38). The woodwinds take over in measure 38 and lead to measure 42, where a viola solo begins (Example 4). The solo, accompanied by held notes in the brass and tremolos in the woodwinds, consists primarily of arpeggiations marked "sul ponticello." The section seems to be a deliberate allusion to Berlioz's *Harold in Italy* (Mvt. 2, meas. 324–334). Chadwick included many features in his own work which closely resemble techniques employed by the French master, but nowhere is there an explicit homage to Berlioz more obvious than here. As with Bizet's work mentioned above, we may be cer-

Example 3. *Sinfonietta,* mvt. 2, meas. 1–8.

Example 4. *Sinfonietta,* mvt. 2, meas. 44–50.

tain that Chadwick was familiar with much of Berlioz's work, including *Harold in Italy*; it was performed by the Boston Symphony Orchestra no fewer than seven times between 1884 and 1903.[2]

Section 2 presents a theme closely related to that encountered in Section 1. It is played by the woodwinds and accompanied by the rest of the orchestra. There is a martial character to the music, due to the introduction in this movement of the trumpet (meas. 51), tambour militaire (meas. 59), and triangle (meas. 67), each of which performs marchlike figures, and piccolo (meas. 55). Although it is unlikely that Chadwick was familiar with the music of Mahler, the entire section certainly resembles passages in some of the works of the Austrian master: the militaristic style, the instrumentation, and the constant crescendo and decrescendo in the pizzicato strings. This is also the area that most closely resembles the farandole movement of Bizet's *L'Arlesienne,* as mentioned earlier. Not only is there a similarity of orchestration throughout the movement, but the melodic contours are also strikingly similar (see Bizet, *L'Arlesienne* Suite No. 1, meas. 1–5).

The section is harmonically conservative until a transitional area is reached in measure 67. At that point the music sounds a dominant-seventh chord of D. After establishing that key, it then returns to the major tonic (A major) in measure 83, where the theme (cf. meas. 51) reappears. The music progresses again to D major in measure 97. A descending bass line beginning on D (meas. 99) leads to Section 3.

The final part begins in measure 104, marked by the return to A minor. The theme is played by the violas and cellos to the accompaniment of woodwinds marked "sotto voce." It is answered as it was earlier (cf. meas 16), but by the upper strings rather than by the winds. The transitional material (cf. meas. 30) returns in measure 134, played by the flute and bassoon. The music progresses to measure 141, where an important passage that emphasizes a descending figure and additive procedures occurs in the string section.

The final section (cf. meas. 41) starts at measure 144, where the tonic arrives. In the next measure the viola solo reappears, accompanied, as before, by tremolos and held notes in the winds and brass. The viola solo finishes its arpeggio figures in measure 153. There follows an unusual post-cadential progression in the woodwinds in measure 154: the minor subdominant (meas. 154–155) is followed by the major submediant (meas. 155–156), the major subdominant (meas. 156), and finally the tonic. Upon reaching the tonic, the horns continue with a remnant of the theme of Part 2 (cf. meas. 51). Marked "in lontananza," it is a wistful passage that brings the movement to a close in A major in measure 162.

Movement 3

The third movement of the *Sinfonietta* is a three-part construction in F major (see Diagram 5–3).

Diagram 5–3. Formal Structure of Third Movement.

Section 1

Theme:	A							T	
Key:	F:ii^7	vi^7	IV	I	V	V	Aug^6	E:I	I
MM.:	1	2	3	4	12/13	14	20	22	25
Comment:									

Theme:	T	A					k		
Key:	F:V^7	ii	vi	IV	I	V	I		I
MM.:	30	38	39	40	41	47	48	51	53
Comment:								Aug^4 in bass	Alla Coda

Section 2

Theme:	B						B	
Key:	B♭:I	I	iii	A:I^6_4	D♭:I	G-C-F-B♭-E♭:I		I
MM.:	54	60	69	71	76	87	92	98
Comment:	Ob.							

Theme:						k			
Key:	V	G♭	Aug^6	D:I	B♭:V	I	V	Aug^6	d:vii^{o7}
MM.:	104	107	108	109	111	112	113	115	116
Comment:							hem.		

				Section 3	Coda	
Theme:		A	A			
Key:	i		iv^6/d	V/F:	I	I
MM.:	118	120	121	122	123	129
Comment:			ferm.	D.S. 1–54		

Titled "Scherzino" and marked "Vivacissimo e leggiero," the third movement begins without introduction. The primary theme, a fine example of Mendelssohnian scherzo style (Example 5), is a playful, quick-moving melody. The movement is somewhat unusual for its employment of both $\frac{9}{8}$ meter and $\frac{3}{4}$ meter from the beginning, and demonstrates Chadwick's interest in syncopation and cross rhythms (see also *Symphonic Sketches,* mvt. 1, meas. 282). After beginning with the minor supertonic (meas. 1), the tonic appears in measure 4. Generally, the section is harmonically conservative. In measure 12 there is a cadence on the dominant, and a clarinet solo begins. The solo is accompanied by the strings,

Example 5. *Sinfonietta,* mvt. 3, meas. 1–5.

which provide the harmonic underpinning; the woodwinds answer the solo in dialogue fashion. After an inverted augmented-sixth chord (meas. 19) the harmony turns to E major in measure 21. This marks the beginning of a transitional section, which features an oboe solo. The theme at this point is simple, in comparatively long-note values, in a folksong style. The texture of the accompaniment is thin. The strings, reintroduced in measures 24–25, continue the melody in measure 29 and lead eventually to the return of the main theme (meas. 37). A closing area begins in measure 47 on the tonic, and, after a large hemiola (meas. 50–51), the first part ends in the tonic in measure 52.

Section 2, in B-flat major and marked "Un poco meno mosso," begins in measure 54. It presents a new melody in the oboe (Example 6), played to the accompaniment of the remaining woodwinds (except the flutes). The melody is a rustic tune, folklike and languishing, that soon makes its way to the flutes in F major (meas. 65) and the clarinets in A major (meas. 71). The quick modulation to such a remote key adds a wonderful dimension of freshness; the delicate scoring of woodwinds and strings throughout this section also adds to the feeling. The tonality again shifts upward by a third to D-flat major in measure 76, where the bassoons and the first cellos play the melody. The harp also enters, while the strings are scored in such a way as to give the section a very rich, thick texture. Here the second cellos and bassoons double the bass part, while the remaining strings, the first cellos, divided violas, and divided violins contribute to this full scoring. This technique is not uncommon in Chadwick's works; often the composer carefully manipulates doublings and divided parts when the impression of a very large orchestra is desired. In measure 87 the music descends through the circle of fifths, beginning on G, finally progressing to E-flat major (meas. 92) and the secondary theme (cf. meas. 53), played by the clarinet. The closing of this section starts in measure 112 in B-flat major. Hemiola occurs in

Example 6. *Sinfonietta.* mvt. 3, meas. 53–56.

measure 113 in the woodwinds and is taken up by the strings in measure 114. The section comes to an end in measure 121, but not before a fragment of the theme associated with the first part is sounded by the first violins (meas. 119).

The third part of this Scherzino is the literal repetition of Section 1. A brief coda (seven measures), marked "Animato assai" and beginning in measure 123, provides a rousing finish in F major.

Movement 4

The fourth movement of the *Sinfonietta* begins with a long introduction. Marked "Assai animato," it begins in an unusual way, in that the first chord of the movement is the minor submediant, or B minor. In what turns out to be a large introductory crescendo to the exposition of this sonata-form movement, the music descends through the circle of fifths (see Diagram 5–4).

Diagram 5–4. Formal Structure of Fourth Movement.

				Part 1 Section			
Theme:	O (Intro.)			P			
Key:	D:vi	E:V—I	A:V—I	D:I	vi	E:V^7 I	C-D-E-F-
MM.:	1	10 11	22 23	37	41	44 45	47
Comment:	crescendo						ascend. bass

			Section 2					
Theme:			S^1					
Key:	G^b-A^b-B^b	V^4_2/F:	V/ii	I	V/vi	V/iii	iii	Aug^6
MM.:	52	56–57	58	62	66	69	70	71
Comment:	ped.							

							Part 2 Section 3		
Theme:		S^2					O		
Key:	iii	V^4_2	V^4_2	V^7/N	N	V^7/F	f:i	i^6	V^6/ii
MM.:	72	74	78	80	84	90	97	101	103
Comment:									

Theme:				P						
Key:	g:V^7	i	V^7/V	c:i	A$^\flat$:IV	I	G$^\#$	G$^\#$	V^7/f	vii^{o7}/D
MM.:	106–7		116	117	122–23		124–31		132	136
Comment:					fugato		enharm.			

						Section 4			
Theme:		T				S^1			
Key:		G	B$^\flat$	g:i$^6_4$	D:iv^7	V/ii	ii	IV	I^6
MM.:	137	139	143	147	160	170	171	173	174
Comment:	G.P.					(cf. meas. 58)			

Theme:		(S^2)							S^2	
Key:	I	V	V$^4_2$	i	V	V^7——	——	V^7	I	
MM.:	176	186	189	192	202	205	208	209	210	212–13
Comment:				minor		hem.		ferm.		Chad. trans.

						Coda			
Theme:					k				
Key:	$^\flat$VI	$^\flat$VI			vi^{o7}	I	IV I	iv I	I
MM.:	214	218	223	227	233	243	250–51	254–55	260
Comment:			Aug^4	Aug^4					

E major is reached in measure 11, followed by A major (meas. 23), and finally the exposition begins in D at measure 37. In addition to its harmonic instability, the music achieves its introductory character by not employing a real theme, but rather presenting a "moto perpetuo" line in the strings, accompanied only lightly by the rest of the orchestra. Furthermore, the dynamics clearly articulate the modulations by the markings that begin each new area; for example, the movement begins pianissimo, E major begins piano, A major begins piano, and D begins fortissimo. A descending bass (E–D–C sharp–C natural–B–B flat–A–G) line begins in measure 31 to produce the final lead-in to the exposition.

The theme associated with the principal key is played by the first violins and the clarinet in measure 37 (Example 7). It is a spirited melody, well-fitted for a finale movement. Again, Chadwick's love for melodies that encompass a large range and are rhythmically animated is perfectly represented in this theme. The

Example 7. *Sinfonietta,* mvt. 4, meas. 37–40.

accompaniment is characterized by sharply punctuated eighth and sixteenth notes in the winds and percussion. At measure 45 the music cadences on E major, and then follows an ascending bass line (C to B flat) in measure 47. After a third-inversion dominant-seventh chord in F major (meas. 56–57), the next section starts in measure 58.

The theme associated with the secondary key is in F major, not the expected dominant. Chadwick had avoided the traditional tonic-dominant relationship before, for example in the first movement of his *Symphonic Sketches,* opting instead to move to the mediant. Obviously, by his decision to employ a tertian relationship rather than the more usual tonic-dominant relationship, the composer was forced to create dramatic movement in ways other than simply by harmonic movement.

A lilting, driving melody, is played by the violins (Example 8). This section, marked "con anima" and in $\frac{6}{8}$ meter, is one of Chadwick's most rhythmically complex, with two metrical divisions sounding simultaneously. The composer has employed mixed meters previously (cf. mvt. 1, meas. 49–54), but nowhere has it occurred with such concentration. In the first four measures duple divisions are played by the second horns and second violins, while the rest of the orchestra presents triple divisions of the beat.

Example 8. *Sinfonietta,* mvt. 4, meas. 56–62.

At measure 64 the theme employs duple beat divisions, while the texture of the accompaniment gradually begins to thicken.

A new area of the secondary section begins in measure 74, where a new idea sounds in the flutes and oboes. The section is further articulated by the appearance of the harp and the triangle, while the pizzicato strings accompany. The scoring of this new area conjures images of the previous "Scherzino" movement, but while it is texturally related, the actual themes are different. The dominant of the Neapolitan (D flat) is played in measure 80, and this leads to the Neapolitan (G flat) in measure 84. At this point the rhythm takes leave of its $\frac{6}{8}$ pulse and shifts to $\frac{3}{4}$. In measure 90 it resumes its $\frac{6}{8}$ division on the dominant of F and leads directly into the development section (meas. 97).

The development begins with a statement of the moto perpetuo figures from the opening of this movement. This introductory material dominates the development, rather than the themes associated with the primary or secondary key, because it is simply easier to manipulate the sixteenth-note figures than the longer themes. The pattern continues until measure 117, where the basses begin playing fragments of the main theme. They are closely followed by imitation in other groups; the second violins and violas take up the fragment in measure 118 and are followed by the first violins in measure 119. The music continues to exploit this material until measure 137. Modulations occur frequently, beginning with F minor (meas. 97), followed by G minor (meas. 107), C minor (meas. 117), A-flat major (meas. 123), and finally a diminished-seventh chord built on C-sharp (meas. 136) before a grand pause is reached in measure 137.

What follows in measure 138 is a recitativelike passage that had appeared earlier, if only briefly, in Chadwick's symphonic style. His penchant for using the strings in this style was first seen in *Symphonic Sketches* (cf. mvt. 4, meas. 215) in a more extended passage than is found here. The declamatory section takes the music to G minor in measure 147. The harp adds to the rich texture at this point. A static subdominant seventh chord in D is reached at measure 160.

The recapitulation begins in measure 170, but the theme presented here is that associated with the secondary key (cf. meas. 58), not the principal-key melody. A similar structural irregularity had occurred in the first movement of the present work (meas.

194). The orchestration is roughly the same as it was at the last presentation of the secondary theme; the woodwinds carry the theme, rather than the first violins, and there is slightly more activity in the winds. The section is harmonically interesting, presenting the submediant (meas. 179) and the mediant (meas. 182), before progressing to the dominant (meas. 186). The tonic minor is reached in measure 192 and the dominant in measure 202. Four measures of hemiola (meas. 205–208) lead to a dominant-seventh chord and a fermata in measure 209.

Material from the secondary tonal area enters in measure 210 (cf. meas. 74) in the tonic, D major. The section displays a slight ambiguity between B-flat major (meas. 214 and 218) and the tonic, exhibiting a dominant relationship to the original presentation of the secondary material, in F major (cf. meas. 58). Forceful tritones are stated in measures 223 and 227. The closing area, beginning in measure 233, is marked by several important characteristics: The composer once again created very dense textures by intricately weaving together several rhythmic patterns. Included are quarter notes, offbeat eighth notes, triplet figures, and grace notes. The section is brought to a close on the dominant in measure 242.

The coda, marked "Presto," revolves almost entirely around the tonic, although the post-cadential coloring on the minor subdominant sounds in measures 250 and 254. This last section is typically Chadwickian, consisting of a quick tempo, scalar flourishes (meas. 251–253), and a rousing finale style.

CRITICAL RECEPTION

Among his orchestral works the *Sinfonietta* ranks as one of Chadwick's most successful ventures in terms of form, clarity, and general appeal. Its craftsmanship, tuneful melodies, and hints of exoticism all contribute to making this work one of the gems of the American repertoire, but curiously it is almost completely unknown.

Contemporary music critics by and large realized the value of the composition. One such reviewer, who obviously thought very highly of the work, commented at length about the composer and his reputation, but his discussion of the composition itself is, to say the least, brief:

> In the Sinfonietta, his latest work, Mr. Chadwick has perhaps reached his high water mark. He has, at all events, been content to forget that, a pupil of Rheinberger, he can write admirable counterpoint, and thus has depended on his own individuality. Mr. Chadwick seems preeminently a composer of scherzos and brilliant finales. In this line he has something personal to say, and a distinctly personal way of saying it, very far removed from the commonplace which he is like to approach in his slow music, and also far away from an imitation of German orthodox composers, of which so much of our American effort consists. In Mr. Chadwick's compositions where a keen sense of rhythm, humor, briliancy and warmth of emotion have play, as in the scherzino and finale of the sinfonietta, the sketches called Jubilee and the Vagrom Ballad, and the vivace and finale of the symphony, we at last have music by an American composer that is more than skilful, intelligent, earnest work after the pattern of French and German musicians who happen to be in the fashion. These movements just mentioned are as distinctive, as peculiarly "American," one may say, as Richard Strauss's music is peculiarly German, as d'Indy's is French. Any European critic, hearing these pieces without knowing who wrote them, would [not] at once infer that their composer came from Munich or Berlin, as has so often been the case with compositions by Americans.[3]

The music critic for the *Boston Herald,* also in attendance at the 1904 performance, wrote of the work even more enthusiastically:

> First of all, it is of a cheerful nature, and few composers have the courage to be gay or hopeful in these days of musical pessimism. It is frankly tuneful, it is well rhythmed, it has vitality. Mr. Chadwick's technical ability has long been recognized; it is of such marked degree that he can afford to be simple in expression, and, when he chooses to display his technique, it is not merely to prove his ability, but to gain effects by a natural and logical process.[4]

The critic has a good deal more to say:

> Furthermore, this new work smacks of the soil. It is not necessary here to raise the question of what constitutes American expression in music or whether such expression be pos-

> sible. It may be said that certain characteristics associated with the American are salient in this sinfonietta—a directness of speech, an undisguised liking for simple sentiment, a peculiar humor, a gayety [*sic*] that approaches recklessness and snaps fingers, a common-sense dealing with aesthetic problems. This music is human, virile. It contains the elements of legitimate popularity. The quality of the melody, when it seems exotic, suggests the negro's tune and rhythm, but not so much in the Dvorakian [*sic*] manner as in what might be called the post-Dvorakian [*sic*] style.[5]

Yet another critic in attendance at the premiere performance wrote his impressions of the *Sinfonietta,* but considered the work only very briefly:

> The Sinfonietta was heard for the first time, and also shows the composer in his free and untrammeled vein—what Beethoven would have called "aufgeknoepft." There is in this work a melodic grace and a directness that call for praise. We like its first movement best. In this there is a subordinate theme that is one of the most charming Oriental bits imaginable. The second movement is remarkably martial—for a canzonetta, and has drums and all the panoply of war. The Scherzino pleased us less, in spite of its pastoral trio.[6]

The *Sinfonietta* received a minor revival in 1910, with performances in New York and Boston. The New York concert prompted one reviewer to examine Chadwick's composition against the background of trends that were popular in contemporary music halls. The writer, having just written a lengthy essay about music of the Baroque period, continues,

> One thing seems tolerably certain and that is that many of these old pieces possess more than a historical interest. Curiously enough this is coming to be felt more now than it was twenty years ago. Then no one could have enjoyed archaic music as much as he can to-day [*sic*]. But the dire tangles and appalling ugliness of much of the problem music now hurled at our patient heads by the troublemakers of France and Germany cause us to turn with eager spirits to the naive and dainty fancies of the old masters, who had no philosophical questions to discuss, no spiritual diseases to analyze, but who were content simply to make music and invite

> us to loaf and permit our souls to bask in the sunlight of beautiful sound.
>
> For this very reason one sat up and rejoiced a few days ago when a sinfonietta [*sic*] by George Chadwick was played. The amiable and gifted American composer put forward a work in which there was no pitfall for the unwary, no concealed meanings, no pathological or other -ological [*sic*] subtleties, but just a bit of lovely musical landscape, filled with the sunshine of a happy disposition and vocal with the songs of spontaneous fancy.
>
> If Mr. Chadwick had been a German he doubtless would have felt it his solemn duty to scoff at diatonic harmonies and the shopworn custom of writing trombone parts for the trombone. In these days we dally only with exotic scales, and for trombones we write piccolo parts, while for trumpets we jot down suggestive little passages quasi-pizzicato or pen a rollicking conceit of muted contra-bass [*sic*] tubas doubled with sarrusaphones and E flat clarinets.[7]

The *Sinfonietta* was again performed by the Boston Symphony Orchestra on February 11, 1910, this time at a matinee concert. According to the critic of the *Boston Journal,* whose article appears under the rubric "Sinfonietta by Chadwick Falls Flat," the composition was a dismal failure:

> It is not so interesting a composition as Mr. Chadwick's "Symphonic Sketches," heard at Symphony concerts two years ago this month. It is not so remarkable either for charm of theme or for strength of general interest. Usually Mr. Chadwick's works have an attractiveness well sustained from beginning to end. Yesterday the interest of the audience rose and fell. Many people went out after the third movement, and at the close of the performance the applause was perfunctory. There was no calling for the composer. The plain fact is that the sinfonietta fell flat.[8]

The well-known music critic Olin Downes heard the 1910 performance and wrote of it for the *Boston Post*. He was much happier with the composition than the *Boston Herald* writer had been, and his compliments remind one of the favorable criticism the work received in 1904:

> Mr. Chadwick's little symphony was heard for the first time at these concerts. Form aside, he might well have dubbed the genial composition, "Novelette in Four Chapters," for there is surely a fanciful underlying programme. Yet the four movements have coherency of thought and style which is genuinely symphonic to a far greater degree than the "Symphonic Sketches" played under Dr. Muck in 1908.
>
> The material and the workmanship of this "sinfonietta" is light and transparent, though scored for full modern orchestra. The pieces are in the nature of a divertimento. There is consistent employment of some material that has an Oriental twang, but these sighs and roulades need not be taken too seriously. The slow movement is pretty, and it has imaginative touches. The growth of the song theme into a march is not merely a thing on paper; it is immediately appreciable to those who listen for the first time, and the dying echo of the march in the last measures is poetic. The scherzo is characterized by clever and diverting rhythms and instrumentation. In this movement, and in the last, Mr. Chadwick's valuable trait of native humor is prominent.[9]

Downes went on in his review to point out similarities he perceived between the scherzo movement of the *Sinfonietta* and the last movement of the *Symphonic Sketches,* writing,

> Whether this section was penned before the finale of the Symphonic Sketches, or not, is unknown to the writer, but at any rate, there is strong affinity between the concluding measures of the two pieces, and there is further resemblance to the "thought of 30 days" in certain poignant measures which interrupt the brillancy of the finale. Yet a further resemblance; in spite of mock Orientalism the prevailing character of the music, with its lively, snappy motives, is a little Scotch and more plain, home-brewed American.[10]

The music critic from the *Boston Monitor* chose to concentrate his efforts on the concert's main feature, a symphony by Anton Bruckner. Of Chadwick's composition he wrote only that

> The Sinfonietta, confessed by its name to be a diminutive work, is full of pretty passages of instrumentation; its purling,

> babbling music came pleasantly after the roaring, foaming music of the symphony.[11]

The critic of the *Boston Evening Transcript* considered the *Sinfonietta* to have considerably more going for it than simply being pretty. In fact, if it had just been pretty, perhaps the audience would not have reacted as the reviewer has reported:

> Mr. Chadwick's Sinfonietta was the other and contrasting piece. It is light music, as the music of the symphony concerts goes—easy to understand, brief, interesting and spirited. Yet it waked little more applause than did Bruckner's unsparing lengths and insistent idiosyncrasies. Worse still—for a very rare occurrence at the afternoon concerts in Mr. Fiedler's time—departures [by the audience] were audible, visible and plentiful at every pause in the music.[12]

The writer believed that he knew why the audience did not appreciate Chadwick's composition. In several statements that reek of gender chauvinism, he continues:

> Perhaps one reason is not far to seek. Mr. Chadwick, in recent years, has written eminently masculine music. The qualities that give it exceptionally an American savor—its robustness, its elasticity, its high spirits, its unexpectedness, its alternate reliance and frankness—are masculine qualities. In a time and a world that is sadly feminized in the arts in America, Mr. Chadwick has dared to write as a man for men. His courage praises him; the music that he has con [*sic*] conceived, like the "Symphonic Sketches" of the spring of 1908 and the "Sinfonietta" of yesterday, praise him still more. Yet all this brings its consequences. Women seemed not to like the Sketches overmuch; they drifted away from the "Sinfonietta," or they applauded it only mildly. Fortunately, tonight, Mr. Chadwick will have more listeners of his own sex. They ought to champion him.[13]

Also in 1910, Walter Damrosch conducted a performance of the *Sinfonietta* with his New York Symphony. An anonymous critic for the *New York Sun* was present at the concert, and displayed a fair knowledge of Chadwick and his music. He wrote:

> Mr. Chadwick, one of the not too numerous band of serious composers who are Americans, wrote in 1904 a Sinfonietta in D Major and this was the novelty of yesterday's list. Mr. Chadwick has been distinguished by a vein of humor and a disinclination to fight out large moral or economic issues in his music.[14]

The writer went on to discuss the music in generally approving terms, but, as one might have guessed, he did not avoid a few subtle critical comments:

> This Sinfonietta is characteristically sane, frank and unpretentious. Its first movement is built on a theme in triple rhythm that Mendelssohn might have been glad to own, a vigorous and well proportioned bit of melody which endured well the frequent repetition insisted upon by the composer. The second movement, with its ingratiating canzonetta, sung chiefly by the wood wind [*sic*] instruments, exemplified the composer's ingenuity in modulation, for after establishing the key of A minor so firmly that the listener forgot all else he led the way to an effective pianissimo conclusion in D major. Lightness of touch and dexterous rhythmic manipulation marked the third division, a scherzino, with a trio section employing the wood wind [*sic*] as a foil to the dominating insistence of the strings in the opening and closing portions, while the finale was animated, without having much of significance to say.[15]

Again, the critic noted Chadwick's proficiency in the composition of lighter movements, and made yet another reference to Mendelssohn.

Finally, the writer closed his review with accolades for the work, which suggest great satisfaction and perhaps a nostalgic pleasure with the results:

> Wholesome music this and well written, not shunning modern harmonic dissonances, yet without a touch of the strained seeking for effect that marks too much of what is written nowadays. Mr. Chadwick may not escape the charge of having an old fashioned musical outlook, but probably this does not seriously disturb him. He was not present yesterday, so far as the audience could discover, to enjoy the applause that greeted his music, which Mr. Damrosch and the orchestra played with spirit and proficiency.[16]

CHAPTER 9

SUITE SYMPHONIQUE IN E^{b} MAJOR

HISTORY

Although Chadwick continued to compose a significant number of orchestral works after his *Suite Symphonique* in 1909, including the symphonic fantasy *Aphrodite* (1912), and his well-received orchestral ballad *Tam O'Shanter* (1915), his abandonment of four-movement, symphonylike compositions upon the completion of the suite was total. The reasons for this are unclear, but given the differing levels of success that he achieved with his symphonies, it is possible that he was simply discouraged.

As with the previous quasi-symphonies, the forms that Chadwick used in the present work are traditional. The first movement, "Allegro molto animato," is a sonata form in E flat, while movement 2, "Romanza," is a five-part form in B flat. The third movement, "Intermezzo-Humoreske-Intermezzo," is cast in a three-part form also in B flat, and the last movement, "Finale," is a sonata form in the tonic, E flat.

This composition, like the earlier *Symphonic Sketches,* requires a rather large orchestra. It is scored for three flutes (one doubling piccolo), paired oboes, clarinets, and bassoons, and one alto saxophone. The brass section consists of four horns, three each of trumpets and trombones, and one tuba. Chadwick expanded the timbral possibilities of his orchestra by including a large percussion battery, consisting of timpani, snare drum, bass drum, cymbals, triangle, glockenspiel, and xylophone. The work also includes a full complement of strings and harp.

The *Suite Symphonique* was first sketched in 1905 and 1906 and completed in 1909. It was not performed until March 29, 1911, when the Philadelphia Orchestra played it under the direction of

Figure 3. Title page, *Suite Symphonique.*

the composer. Chadwick had entered his suite in a composition competition sponsored by the National Federation of Music Clubs. The suite took first prize for "best orchestral work," and the composer was awarded the considerable sum of $700 and a performance by the esteemed orchestra.[1] Dedicated to "Frederick A. Stock and the Theodore Thomas Orchestra in Chicago," the suite had its New England premiere by the Boston Symphony Orchestra on April 13, 1911, with Chadwick conducting.

ANALYSIS

Movement 1

The first movement of the *Suite Symphonique* is marked "Allegro molto animato," and is cast in sonata form (see Diagram 6–1).

Diagram 6–1. Formal Structure of First Movement.

		Part 1 Section 1										
Theme:		P^1				P^2				P^1	P^2	P^2
Key:	$E^b:I^6$	I^6	I	V/V	V	V	$V/G^b:V$		I	I	Aug^6	$g:i^6$
MM.:	1	2	6	14	15	16	18	20	21	23	27	31
Comment:						clar. solo.						

Theme:	P^1/P^2		P^2		t^1		t^2		
Key:	$B^b:I$		Aug^6	g:i	$G^b:I$	I^6	G:V	vii^{o9}	vii^4_3
MM.:	35	40	43	44	52	56	60	72	76
Comment:		brass							

	Section 2							Part 2 Section 3	
Theme:	S				(S)				P^2
Key:	I	A:V	I	$E:I^6$	I	$d:iv^6$	i	A^{b4}_3	
MM.:	77	84	85	93	95	108	109/10	111	113
Comment:									

Theme:			t^3		t^1		t^1	t^3
Key:	E^{b9}	b^{b4}_2	$B^b:I^6$	V	I	$G^b:I^6$	$D^b:I$	$A:I^6$
MM.:	127–28		135	146	148	160	166	178
Comment:						sync.		

Theme:	N^1	N^1					
Key:	b^b:i^6	$c^\#$:i^6_4		Aug^6	E:ii^{o7}-I	I	A^b:V
MM.:	190	195	201	211	222	224	230
Comment:			B ped.				

	Part 4								
Theme:	P^1		P^2	t^2		(S)			N^2
Key:	E^b:I	I	I		Aug^6	C:I	A:ii$^{o4}_2$	I	I
MM.:	238	251	252	271	287	288	303	304–06	
Comment:						$\frac{4}{4}$			$\frac{6}{4}$

Theme:			(S)				t^3		
Key:	D	g	vii^{o7}/C	vii^{o7}/F	Aug^6	G^b	B^b	E^{b6}	G:ii
MM.:	314	321	322	326	334	339	346	349	360
Comment:			sync.						Chad. trans.

							Coda	
Theme:		P^1		P^1	t^4		(S)	
Key:	I	I	A:I		E:I^6_4	Aug^6	I	I
MM.:	362	364	367	370	384	392	399	416
Comment:								

The movement begins with a one-measure introduction, consisting of an E-flat major scale in the harp and strings, which leads to the first theme associated with the principal key (P^1). The theme, a syncopated, somewhat fanfarelike opening, is played by the bassoons, cellos, and upper brass instruments. This combination of instruments makes for a very brilliant, colorful exposition (Example 1). The strings answer the first idea in measures 6–9 before the section reaches another scalar lead-in, this time on the scale of B-flat major (cf. meas. 1), which progresses to the second theme associated with the tonic (P^2).

Example 1. *Suite Symphonique,* mvt. 1, meas. 2–5.

The second principal theme is played by a solo clarinet (Example 2), which sounds above a thinly scored string section, although a brief moment of dialogue occurs with the second violin. All other instruments are omitted at this point, making for a very stark contrast with the heavier scoring of the earlier measures. The theme itself is closely related to the first theme, having the same general shape, and only a slightly different character, the former being festive, the latter more pensive. After the clarinet plays the initial phrase, it is answered by the upper woodwinds (meas. 21) before several melodic ideas spread throughout the texture. An augmented-sixth chord in measure 27 carries the music to the key of G minor in measure 31, where the second principal theme appears in the woodwinds. In measure 35 two variations of both principal themes occur in B-flat major. The lower strings present a slight variation of the first principal theme, while the first violins play a theme loosely based on the second. This material continues to measure 39, were the brass section is prominent in presenting a fortissimo passage of quarter notes that lead to another sounding of G minor (meas. 44). After passing through a series of borrowed chords, the music reaches a transitional section in measure 52.

Beginning in G-flat minor, the section introduces a new, startling style. It is marked "poco tranquillo," and features a solo clarinet, lightly accompanied by upper brass, woodwinds, and harp. The strings enter in measure 54 with a syncopated rhythm that will later become an important feature of the movement. The transitional area continues in measure 60 on the dominant of G major. It remains lightly scored, and is marked "calmato ed espressivo assai," featuring the melody played in the horns.

The music reaches the secondary area, in G major and marked "Molto meno mosso e largamente," in measure 77. As in the *Symphonic Sketches* and *Sinfonietta,* here the secondary area occurs in the mediant rather than in the dominant area. The theme associated with the new tonality is found in the flutes and violas. The

Example 2. *Suite Symphonique,* mvt. 1, meas. 16–19.

melody, one of the composer's less inspired inventions, is very awkward, not particularly effective nor memorable. It begins successfully with the entrance in measure 77 and progresses to measure 78, where triplets are introduced. The following musical material, in duple rhythm, is clumsy and seems forced for the folksong style that the theme otherwise suggests. The music modulates to A major (meas. 85) before progressing to E major (meas. 95), where a variation of the secondary theme appears in the woodwind section. The exposition gradually draws to a close after a plagal cadence on D minor (meas. 110).

Chadwick has obviously altered his thought about traditional harmonic procedures in this work. By ending an exposition that begins in E flat on a D minor sonority, the composer has all but signaled to listeners that he is no longer concerned with conventional harmonic practice. Rather, the themes are of the utmost concern in the present suite, and therefore the most significant elements of the dramatic structure are the melodies and the sudden impact of harmonies employed for their shock value, as evidenced in the development.

The development begins (meas. 111) in stark contrast to the music that immediately preceded it; the first chord is a strangely out-of-place second-inversion A-flat seventh chord, expressed in lively, rumbalike rhythm. Themes related by inversion to the second primary-key theme (P^2, cf. meas. 44) appear frequently. The music reaches a transitional section in measure 135, in the key of B flat. A new area is reached in measure 148, which presents an augmented version of the earlier transitional theme (from measure 52), stated in the violins and horn. The static nature of the augmented melody contrasts with a wealth of rhythmic activity throughout the brass and lower woodwind parts. The rumba figures appear again in measure 160, before the development progresses to D-flat major, where the augmented theme reappears. The key of A major is reached in measure 178, marked by the entrance of the tambour militaire. Soon, the remaining instruments in the large battery of percussion enter, and melodic material in B-flat minor is presented by the trombones and tuba in measure 190. This takes the music to C-sharp minor (meas. 195), where the trombones and tuba repeat the earlier statement (meas. 190). A pedal on B extends from measure 201 to measure 208. An unusually prominent augmented-sixth chord sounds in measure 211, followed by a brass chorale section that features an augmented version of the previous one (cf. meas. 40). After brief sections of E major (meas. 222–225) and C minor (meas. 226–229), the music progresses to E flat (meas. 230), although the key at this point remains somewhat ambiguous because the tonic triad is in second inversion and the minor seventh (D flat) sounds prominently. The E-flat tonality becomes somewhat more focused when the harmony is presented in root position (meas. 234).

The recapitulation begins in measure 238 in the tonic key. The melody is scored for smaller forces than was the case at the beginning of the movement; here the trumpets are omitted while clarinets are added. In measure 252 the second principal-key theme (P^2), stated in the exposition earlier by the clarinet, is sounded by the flute. The syncopated rhythms reappear in measure 257 and continue through 263. At this point the melodic material dominates in a dialogue fashion; it appears in the clarinet (meas. 263), the horn (meas. 264), and the violins (meas. 267). A transitional section in measures 271 to measure 288 leads to a slight variation of the secondary theme (see meas. 77) in C major. This passage is an excellent example of the dense texture that the composer sometimes preferred to write for the string section. While the forces are small (woodwinds, horns, and strings) they produce a very rich sound. The key of A major is reached in measure 304, and in measure 306 a new theme occurs, in $\frac{6}{4}$ meter. It is a reserved melody, encompassing a narrow range, and bears some resemblance to the secondary theme (cf. meas. 77). The section progresses to the dominant of C major in measure 321, where, rather than bringing the movement to a close, Chadwick introduced a major new developmental area. Marked "con anima," the section begins with rumba rhythms sounded in the strings. Alternated with these rhythms are inverted fragments based on the second primary-key theme (cf. meas. 252). In addition to the thematic development in this passage, the harmonic movement is also very developmental; a diminished chord built on B sounds (meas. 322), followed by a diminished chord on E (meas. 326), a diminished chord on D (meas. 332), and an augmented-sixth chord (meas. 334). G-flat major is reached in measure 339, where the brass section enters, fortissimo, playing a veiled version of the secondary theme. From this point the music progresses through B-flat major (meas. 346), E-flat major (meas. 349), and G major (meas. 362).

In measure 364, the first primary-key theme appears in G major. Later it passes through A major (meas. 367). A Chadwickian transitional passage, beginning in E major (meas. 384), leads to an augmented-sixth chord (meas. 392) and another Chadwickian transition.

The coda is straightforward; in the tonic key it presents material based on the second primary-key theme in the strings and lower woodwinds. The brass and woodwinds present accompaniment figures in a fanfarelike fashion until measure 414. The movement comes to a close at measure 416.

Movement 2

The second movement of the *Suite Symphonique* is subtitled "Romanza" and marked "Andante espressivo." Cast in a five-part form (ABCDA) in the key of B-flat major, it is perhaps most notable for its unusual and colorful instrumentation (see Diagram 6–2).

Diagram 6–2. Formal Structure of Second Movement.

	Part 1					Part 2		
Theme:	A		A			B		
Key:	B^b:I		I	V	I	d:i	G:V^6_5	III
MM.:	1	14	17	24	25–6	27	31	34
Comment:	sax.	ferm.						

					Part 3						
Theme:	T				C			T			
Key:	V^7	B^b:V^7	I	V	I	V	I	e^b	f	F	d:V^7/V
MM.:	35	39	40	42	50	65	66	67	71	76	81
Comment:											

	Part 4			Part 5						
Theme:	D			A			k			
Key:	V	B^b:I^6	IV^9-V	I	V^7	I	I	ii^6_5	I	I
MM.:	82	83	93	94	101	102	110	113	114	117
Comment:			ferm.							

Part 1 begins without introduction in measure 1. It presents the main theme, a nostalgic, songlike melody, played by the saxophone

Example 3. *Suite Symphonique,* mvt., 2 meas. 1–4.

(Example 3), although the score indicates that if that instrument is not available, a cello may substitute. After passing through the dominant (meas. 8), the music halts momentarily on the submediant at a fermata (meas. 14) before progressing to a restatement of the main theme in the violins (meas. 17). The music reaches a climax on a subdominant-ninth chord (E flat, meas. 22), before cadencing and progressing to the next section.

Part 2 begins in measure 27 in the key of D minor. It presents a new melody in the flute and bassoon parts and is accompanied by very active figures in the second violins and violas. At measure 31, the dominant of G major is played and takes the music to measure 35, where a transitional theme appears. The music returns to B-flat major in measure 40, where it remains until the new section begins.

The third part begins in measure 50 with a dialogue among several of the instruments. Beginning in B-flat major, the solo clarinet plays the melody, distinctive for its rhythmic activity and its large range. It is followed by the flute (meas. 52), to begin a section of conversation between the two instruments. The accompaniment here is marked by simple rhythmic figures in the strings, with the saxophone playing a quiet countermelody that is somewhat more subdued and languishing than its earlier theme. Rhythmic activity increases at measure 67, where a transitional area is reached, and fragments of the main melody proceed through F minor (meas. 71), F major (meas. 76), and D minor (meas. 81).

Part 4 (meas. 83) differs considerably from all that has come before. Although it begins in B-flat major, much of the section's tonality is ambiguous. Here again, as in the *Symphonic Sketches* and *Sinfonietta,* there are orientalist traits; frequently varying meters destabilize the rhythmic pulse, and a variety of special effects are employed, including harmonics in the strings, mutes in the brass, and directions to play sotto voce in the woodwinds.

The textures are transparent, the melodies are fluid, and the harmonies are nonfunctional. This combination of elements predominates up to the appearance of a ninth-chord in measure 93, where a saxophone cadenza leads into the final part.

Part 5 begins in measure 94 with a repetition of the main theme. It is again in the tonic key, but instead of the saxophone presenting the melody, it is found in the violins. The music progresses to measure 102, where the harp takes on new prominence and the surrounding accompaniment figures gradually grow in intensity. The cadential tonic chord is sounded in measure 110, where remnants of the main theme are passed throughout the orchestra. The harp reintroduces a hint of exoticism by the use of melodic G flats over a B-flat pedal. The flatted-sixth interval used here gives the entire section the effect of being Phrygian, and the pianissimo dynamic marking adds to an impression of mysticism. The movement ends quietly in measure 117.

Movement 3

The third movement of the Suite, "Intermezzo e Humoreske," is one of Chadwick's most individualistic inventions, a wonderful example of Chadwick's ability to infuse popular styles into symphonic forms. Cast in three distinct parts, the movement begins without introduction in B-flat major (see Diagram 6–3).

Diagram 6–3. Formal Structure of Third Movement.

	Part 1 Intermezzo								
Theme:	P^1								P^1
Key:	Bb:vii^{ø7}	c:V	i	E^b:V^9/V	V	V	V	I	C:I
MM.:	1	7	8	16	17	18	19	20	21
Comment:									

Theme:				T					(P^1)	
Key:	I^6	Aug^6	iv	I	I	V^7	I	B^b:vii$^{ø6}_{5}$	G:I	V
MM.:	31	33	35	36	43	50	51	53	64	87
Comment:								dev.		

									Part 2 Humoreske		
Theme:	(P^1)			T					P^2		
Key:		iv	V	I	I	V	I	V	I	V/V	D:vii^{o7}/V
MM.:	93	111	115	116	122	127	128	131	132	144	147
Comment:								ferm.			

Theme:									t	P^2
Key:	I^6	V^7	I	III	Aug^6	I	Aug^6	I	I	$G^b{:}I^4_2$
MM.:	151	152	153	157	158	159	164	165	167	173
Comment:										

Theme:								
Key:	V	$C^{\#}{:}IV^7$	V^4_2	V	(whole tone mvt.)			$G{:}vii^{o7}$
MM.:	174	176	177	187	188	192	196	205
Comment:					Debussian			
							tuba Yankee Doodle	

Theme:	P^2		P^2						k	
Key:	I	ii				V	I	Aug^6	I	A^{b7}
MM.:	206	209	210	218	225	226	227	232	233	241
Comment:			str.	bsn.	fl.					

		Part 3 (Coda)							
		Intermezzo							
Theme:		P^1			P^1				
Key:	$g{:}V^4_3$	$ii^{\phi 6}_5$	vii^{o7}/V	V	vii^{o7}	V	iv^4_3	III	i^7
MM.:	242	246	252	253	254	257	261	265	267
Comment:				D pedal					

Theme:				k		
Key:	iv	iv^7	iv-V	i	i	i
MM.:	273	276	280	281	287	302
Comment:				(t)		

The first theme is a lilting duet in the lower woodwinds (Example 4). It is accompanied by a transparent, lightly scored string section and the horns. Harmonic development begins immediately; in measure 8 the music arrives in C minor. There follows

Example 4. *Suite Symphonique,* mvt. 3, meas. 1—4.

(meas. 9) a new melodic idea that is gradually developed throughout the movement. The theme progresses to E flat (meas. 20), but leads directly into the key of C major in the following measure (meas. 21). At this point the theme (cf. meas. 9) pervades the music until measure 36, where a transitional theme, in C major, is heard.

The next area of the work is the most developmental of the movement. After a cadence in C major (meas. 50–51), the first sonority of measure 53 is a half-diminished chord built on A. The thematic material employed is the principal theme (cf. meas. 1). By measure 56 the key is B flat, but this harmony is transitional and serves to take the music to the key of G major. At this point (meas. 64) a subtle harmonic ascent from G major begins, through A major (meas. 69) and B major (meas. 74). From here the music takes an unexpected turn to the key of E-flat major (meas. 79), where a transitional theme is stated. The E-flat sonority is a prelude to the arrival of the dominant (D major) in measure 83, which leads to the tonic (meas. 90). From measure 90 there is more development of the same material, and it continues to be played throughout the orchestra. Beginning in measure 105 there is a predominance of Ds, which ultimately lead to the tonic G minor (meas. 116), where the transitional theme reappears. The transition leads to a fermata in measure 131, which brings this part to a close.

Part 2 of the movement, the "Humoreske," begins in measure 132. Marked "Molto robusto," the section is in G major, the major submediant of the opening B-flat major tonality. This, of course, marks another avoidance of the tonic-dominant relationship within a movement. The theme appears in the bassoons and the lower strings.

The humor in this movement lies not only in the unusual orchestration, but also in the highly decorated, clumsy melodic style and the awkward rhythm in $\frac{5}{4}$ meter. The xylophone enters in measure 145. The music progresses to D major in measure 151, where the woodwind section, joined by the harp, takes the music to D major in measure 159. At this point the woodwinds continue their sixteenth-note figures to the accompaniment of a long descending bass line that leads through a complete octave, back to the tonic (D major) in measure 165. A brief transition (meas. 167–172) leads to a return of the main theme of this section (meas. 173). The music modulates to C-sharp major in measure 177, where the main theme still prevails.

The passage beginning in measure 188 displays Chadwick's adeptness at composing in the impressionistic style, although it is not clear whether this parody of Debussy should be understood as complimentary or comical. The section bears all of the characteristic traits of the style: There are several diverse rhythmic layers, including ostinato figures; mystical effects are achieved by the use of sul ponticello in the strings and mutes in the brass; the harmonic movement is nonfunctional; and unusual effects are achieved through the use of instruments that are seldom utilized, at least in solo settings, such as the tuba (meas. 192). Also notable is Chadwick's clever employment of the tune "Yankee Doodle" (meas. 196). A transition begins in measure 199, which takes the music to measure 206, where there is a return of the second principal theme (cf. meas. 132). Unlike the orchestration of the previous section, here the theme is presented by the violins. The woodwind theme (cf. meas. 151) sounds in measure 227 and leads to measure 237, where a somewhat startling change in rhythm takes place, from duple to triple. This is part of a larger written-out ritardando that started in measure 231 with sixteenth notes and progressed to triplets (meas. 237) and finally to eighth notes (meas. 239).

Part 3 is a shortened version of the first part of the movement, "Intermezzo." It begins in the key of G minor, although on an unexpected second-inversion dominant seventh chord. The chord is arrived at by unusual enharmonic and chromatic movement from the previous A-flat-seventh chord (meas. 241); the A flat, C, and G flat of measure 241 progress to A, C, and F sharp, respectively, with the addition of a D. After four introductory measures the primary theme (cf. meas. 1) begins in measure 246. The movement progresses as in the opening section; in measure 281 the transitional material reappears, clearly in G minor, where it remains to the final measures. The movement draws to a quiet close in G minor, following an ethereal ascending violin line that spans more than two octaves.

Movement 4

The final movement of the *Suite Symphonique* is an optimistic, virtuosic composition in E-flat major and cast in sonata form (see Diagram 6–4).

Diagram 6–4. Formal Structure of Fourth Movement.

		Part 1 Section 1						Section 2		
Theme:	O	P			(P)		t^1	S		
Key:	E^b:I^6	I	V/V	V	A:I^6_4	V	I	I	g	a
MM.:	1	5	11	12	18	24	25	29	33	40
Comment:										

					Section 3						
Theme:	K									(P)	t^2
Key:		F:V	I	B^b	a^b	D	F	B^b	e		V/F$^\#$:
MM.:	41—44	44	45	49	51	55	59	63	67	74	84
Comment:	oriental.										

Theme:	N			t^2			O
Key:	I	V	V^6/E^b	g:i	f$^\#$	f$^\#$	A^b:I^6
MM.:	89	105	120	121	139	146	147–50
Comment:						ferm.	

	Section 4								
Theme:	P	t^1		S	K			(P)	t^3
Key:	I	E^b:I	I	vi	D	V	I		
MM.:	151	158	161	162	170	174	178	180	184
Comment:						(Section 3)			

						Coda					
Theme:			S			(P)			(P)		
Key:	D:I	I			V^7	E^b	D^b	A^b	f	I	I
MM.:	194	200	201	206	218	219	226	242	250	264	276
Comment:	D ped.			B^b ped.							

The movement begins with four introductory measures that rapidly build to the first statement of the theme associated with the principal key (meas. 5). The theme, played by the violins, is eminently suited to a finale ending (Example 5). Like many of Chadwick's inventions, the rhythmic vitality of the theme, its changing accentuation, and its extended range suit it well to later manipulation. The music begins to develop by measure 12, where the dominant is reached. Here new rhythmic ideas are played in the

Example 5. *Suite Symphonique,* mvt. 4, meas. 5–8.

woodwinds, and the descending figure derived from the main theme is presented in sequential patterns in the lower strings. In measure 18 the principal theme is again stated, now in the key of A major. At this point the thematic material actually serves as transitional material that leads to the presentation of the secondary theme.

The secondary area begins conservatively (meas. 29.), with the theme stated in the upper woodwinds to accompaniment by the strings (Example 6). In measure 41 the music arrives at another section (cf. *Symphonic Sketches* and *Sinfonietta*) that focuses attention once again on Chadwick's love of the exotic; here one finds a lovely "oriental" melody that emphasizes the tritone (A to E flat). This relationship also outlines the large-scale harmonic movement to this point (E-flat major in meas. 1 to A major in meas. 18). As has been noted in earlier "chinoise" movements by Chadwick, such techniques as sul ponticello, use of harmonics, mutes, and diversity of rhythms all help the composer achieve exotic effects.

This area is brief, lasting only four measures before the development section arrives, although considering the amount of development that has been encountered up to this point, it is some-

Example 6. *Suite Symphonique,* mvt. 4, meas. 29–32.

what misleading to say that the music has reached the development. The section begins somewhat unexpectedly in the key of F major. New thematic material is played by the winds, while motives derived from the theme associated with the principal key are frequently heard in the string section. The music touches on a variety of keys, including B-flat major (meas. 49), A-flat minor (meas. 51), D major (meas. 55), and E-flat minor (meas. 61). A fragment of the principal theme sounds in measure 74, and the dynamic level gradually builds to measure 84, where a transition begins. The transition, relying upon material from the development section, is brief and proceeds to a new section in measure 89.

The new section, marked "Tranquillo," is short and appears strangely out of place. It introduces not only a new theme, but also a new mood, one that seems foreign to the work. In the key of F-sharp major, the section presents a dolorous theme in the horns. Soon it is transferred to the violins (meas. 97), and shortly thereafter it makes its way to woodwinds (meas. 105). From here the music leads directly into the next section following a dominant of E-flat chord in measure 120.

The new section, beginning in measure 121, employs thematic material from the previous section (cf. meas. 89), but it is used more freely. This transitional section, beginning in G minor, leads to fragments of the principal-key theme (meas. 139, cf. meas. 5), played in the lower strings and tuba. An ascending response in the horns (meas. 140–141) leads to a fermata (meas. 142). Another descending figure is played, with the response this time coming from the clarinets and trumpets, and, as before, reaching a fermata (meas. 146).

The recapitulation begins in measure 151 after four measures of introduction as in the opening of the movement. The difference at this point, however, is that rather than being in the tonic the music is in A-flat major, the subdominant. The key of E flat is not reached until a transitional passage (meas. 158), but it is short-lived and leads directly to the theme associated with the secondary key (cf. meas. 29), here in C minor. The sequence of events from this point is generally predictable. The "oriental" inventions reappear (meas. 170–173). In measure 174 the theme associated with the development (cf. meas. 45) is played once again, clearly on the dominant of E flat. At long last the music reaches a firm E-flat major in measure 178; the thematic material, however, is that associated with the development, not the primary theme. The section is very much like the development section proper; it shows a good deal of harmonic ingenuity, fragmentation of themes, and virtuoso orchestration. The music reaches a D pedal in measure 194, which leads to D major (meas. 200). At this point the secondary theme (cf. meas. 29) is played by the strings and woodwinds. A pedal on B flat sounds in measure 206, and this leads to a dominant-seventh of E flat in measure 218.

The coda, marked "Molto vivace," begins in measure 219. As with many of Chadwick's codas, this one is multi-sectional; the first section is rhythmically vibrant, emphasizing dotted figures associated with the principal theme. Harmonically, it is also adventuresome; beginning in E-flat major, it quickly passes through D flat (meas. 226) and A flat (meas. 242).

The second segment of the coda is marked "Molto energico" and begins in F minor. The harmonic rhythm slows drastically as the principal theme is presented in augmentation. In measure 263, a subdominant-seventh chord leads to E-flat major in the following measure. From here the music remains in E flat.

CRITICAL RECEPTION

The *Suite Symphonique* was generally heralded as a success by the local media in Philadelphia, where the work received its premiere performance. Critics commented on many of the aspects of Chadwick's compositional style that had been discussed throughout his career. The reviewer for the *Inquirer* wrote,

> It is a fluently written, skillfully constructed and interesting piece, in four movements, an opening allegro, a Romanza, which constitutes the andante; an intermezzo, which takes the place of the classic scherzo, and a spirited finale, and of these four the third is perhaps the most striking and original. All, however, are well conceived and cleverly executed. Although the texture of the opening allegro is so loose that it communicates an impression of fragmentariness and incoherence which would probably be removed by a better acquaintance with the music, it contains much that is ingratiating and sympathetic and easily holds the attention. The romanza embodies a beautiful theme which undergoes a va-

> riety of effective and illuminating transmutations. There is genuine humor as well as fascinating melody in the intermezzo, and a brilliantly ebullient finale brings the whole to a logical and convincing close. It is all highly attractive, and the suite may be expected to find a frequent and welcome place on the program of the concert room.[2]

The music critic of the *Evening Bulletin* wrote a similar, mostly uncritical review of the composition, stating that it

> . . . is nobly conceived and written with deep and true musicianship on a foundation of pure melody. It has few complexities, for, which by no means superficial, it preserves, in all its most impressive effects, the charm of simplicity and directness. Harp, strings and woodwinds are the prevailing voices, and are used with alluring melodiousness, particularly in the second movement—the Romanze [*sic*], which is the most beautiful of the composition. The Humoreske has a blithesome touch, being true to its classification in the marked air of whimsicality, having for a moment a suggestion that it is about to sing "Yankee Doodle," but, with a touch of mischievous playfulness, quickly turning to something else before the tune can be clearly defined. The finale is on broader lines than the preceding movements, and in its climax prove that Mr. Chadwick is capable of producing the bigger effects, though the brasses, as he handles them, never become blatant, and through all and pervading all still shines the radiant beauty of the melody that gives his worthy prizewinning composition its greatest charm.[3]

It is difficult to understand why the remarks from the Philadelphia critics were so positive. There are, of course, many fine moments in the composition; but some of the more obvious flaws in the work are easily noted on a first hearing and would likely not have been missed by the Boston critics. Perhaps here is another instance (as with the *Sinfonietta*) of the press granting Chadwick some special consideration because of his renown and because, after all, the work had just won a fairly important competition.

What occurred in Philadelphia was not duplicated when the work was finally performed in Boston. On the contrary, the suite's 1911 performance by the Boston Symphony Orchestra was greeted by a long and disapproving article by the well-known music critic Henry T. Parker. In his review Parker makes his views of competitions known and compares the work to Chadwick's earlier *Symphonic Sketches:*

> Mr. Chadwick did not write it for the competition, arranged by the Federation of Musical Clubs in which it lately won a prize. Having the music finished and in hand, he merely submitted it. Yet more than once it does not escape the easy obviousness of prize music, and still more does it suggest an effort to do again what Mr. Chadwick did so interestingly, individually and stirringly in his first Symphonic Suite [*Symphonic Sketches*]. That suite, last played at the Symphony Concerts in Dr. Muck's time, was rich in American spirit and American voice. The listener might hear in it much that was of American sentiment, American humor, American jubilation, of the quick shiftings of mood that are very American, of the frankness of one feeling crowding upon another. Mr. Chadwick's melodic invention was fresh and felicitous; his development and clothing of his material alert, imaginative, high-spirited. The first suite was good to hear in itself, and it was very American music besides.[4]

The esteem in which Parker held *Symphonic Sketches* had no effect on what he thought about the *Suite Symphonique*. Known throughout his career as a tough and direct critic, Parker's initials, H.T.P., often stood for "Hard to Please" or "Hell to Pay" among musicians who knew the damage that he could inflict.[5] Regarding the *Suite,* Parker quickly got to the point:

> The Symphonic Suite of yesterday brought no such agreeable stimulation. Mr. Chadwick's invention of melody flags, and the slow movement, a Romance, barely escapes a rather thin and commonplace sweetness in matter and in manner. It is simplicity and sentiment carried to the perilous verge, even though the instrumental turf be velvety. The "Humoreske," the other middle movement after a pretty little intermezzo, does not much heighten the quality or the interest of the music. Neither the rattle of the xylophone nor the tinkling of the triangle, nor yet again the mockery of Debussian and Pucciniesque dissonances and progressions is in itself amusing. The treatment is everything, and Mr. Chadwick's treatment did not seem musically fresh or musically witty. He took thought and pains at his humor. In the finale,

> he would "jubilate" American-wise, as he did in the lusty vagabond song and the mockery of Bach in the finale of the first Symphonic Suite [*Symphonic Sketches*]. The second thoughts do not match the first: the jovial, lusty, tumbling inspiration will not come. The first movement, distinctly a lyric piece, pleasantly invented, ingeniously and fancifully ordered, relieves, too early, the tameness of the whole. It is a sort of sentimental yet spirited song that American composers from MacDowell onward have sung agreeably, imaginatively. Elsewhere, Mr. Chadwick's music needs freshness, needs spirit, and, above all, brevity.[6]

Parker was correct in many of his claims. The melody often flags in the first movement of the suite, perhaps because Chadwick was trying to do too much in the way of development. The second movement, as Parker claims, is sentimental and reminiscent of music of an earlier age, perhaps a bit dated for the second decade of the twentieth century. Yet, in some respects Parker's judgements seem too harsh. When Chadwick intends the work to be witty, as in the Debussy parody, it is very witty. That kind of humor was also quite fresh. In a time when many composers took the impressionistic style very seriously, Chadwick was bold enough to satirize it. It is true that, overall, the *Suite* does not measure up to the high standards that Chadwick achieved with his *Symphonic Sketches,* but Parker's castigation was excessive.

Chadwick's suite fared much better in New York, where it was performed by the New York Symphony in 1912, with the composer conducting. Here, as in Philadelphia, the work was generally considered a success. Critics were taken by the "jocosity" and the freshness of the new work. The critic of the *New York Times* wrote,

> It is in the form of a symphony; the fact that its content is somewhat lighter and at some moments more jocose than composers are in the habit of putting into a symphony no doubt led the composer to let it go as a suite. The first movement is the most serious of the four, and in its substance and treatment the most interesting. There is an engaging quality of freshness and vigor in its themes, especially the first, and its development is ingenious, yet spontaneous, with taking rhythms and much that is effective in the orchestration. The slow movement is pleasingly, and perhaps rather obviously,

> melodious. The third movement is called "intermezzo and humoresque," and as Mr. Damrosch said in his few words before the concert began, there is something tangible of a humorous nature in the movement to justify the title of "humoresque." A "Cake Walk," in five-four time, and a bit of parody in the modern French style, the "whole tone" scale of Debussy, the consumptive frogs in dismal pools of the decadent poets. The cake walk is not very definitely outlined in the music, though the quintuple rhythm is unmistakable; so is the hint of Debussy, which is scarcely more than a hint. As nothing is easier to parody than this idiom, Mr. Chadwick's self-restraint in the matter is commendable.[7]

The critic closed with praise for Chadwick and what he was trying to accomplish in the *Suite Symphonique*. He concluded,

> But more than these things is the essential gayety and jocose spirit of the music, which require no elucidation. In the last movement there is a return to something more serious, though the energy and spontaneity of the first movement are again felt in it. The suite gave pleasure and was applauded heartily. It discloses a characteristic side of Mr. Chadwick's talent that is most ingratiating, and that has given pleasure before.[8]

An anonymous critic, who was probably in attendance at the same 1912 concert in New York, penned one of the most humorous and insightful reviews that the *Suite Symphonique* received. The critic, unlike so many others, appears to have understood exactly what the composer was trying to do in the composition, stating,

> First of all, Mr. Chadwick appears to have sought to make his music simple and tuneful. He has not indulged in the present fashionable craze for strange scales or weird chords. He has found in elementary materials of music all that was necessary to his amiable purpose, namely to make people happy. This, of course, condemns Mr. Chadwick's suite at once as being destitute of profundity, atmosphere, psychology, metaphysics, pathology, idealism, realism, or even snobbism, which is rampant in art. It is just old-fashioned music. And it is not even pretentious. It does not make believe that it is great. It is content to be merely pleasing.[9]

Although we do not know it for sure, it is likely that, especially in his last three quasi-symphonies, Chadwick's aim was to please, but only himself and his audience. Working to please the critics is, after all, a young composer's game. Knowing that he was in the latter stages of his career and composing in a style that was quickly going out of date, Chadwick, one of the handful of premier composers in the United States, had little reason to care what the critics thought.

The New York critic went on to discuss Chadwick's work, sarcastically writing that "there is something yet worse to be said about it," and then proceeding to state his thoughts about Antonin Dvořák. The critic voiced the minority opinion when he wrote,

> This suite betrays the awful fact that Mr. Chadwick has been bitten by the Dvorak [*sic*] American music insect. He has not hesitated to write intellectual ragtime, such as the Bohemian put into his American Symphony to the intense disgust of Boston. Nor has the distinguished head of the New England Conservatory shrunk from openly imitating the melodic line of the negro tunes.[10]

Apparently Chadwick's use of "intellectual ragtime" did not worry the writer, for he continued,

> At any rate it may be said that it is a pretty suite well worth hearing. The slow movement is perhaps the most fluent but the cleverest in characterization is the intermezzo. The first movement has spots in which the joints are exposed and the instrumentation is thin. But on the whole the composition is well made and well orchestrated.[11]

A final comment is one that had resounded throughout Chadwick's career, but seems to have had little effect on his decision to keep returning to the podium:

> It was commendably played, but would probably have been more effective if directed by the conductor to whom the orchestra was accustomed.[12]

CHAPTER 10

CONCLUSION

HISTORICAL CONSIDERATIONS

Chadwick's symphonic works constitute the most important body of orchestral compositions by an American composer before World War I. They are, in terms of craftsmanship, ingenuity, and sheer quantity, unparalleled. No other American composer before the Great War wrote symphonic music with Chadwick's dedication. From the beginning of his career to nearly the end of his creative activity, he composed symphonic music. Such cannot be said of any of the American symphonists, including those well known and forgotten, who preceded Chadwick.

The complete histories of Chadwick's symphonic works, including their conceptual origins, development, and eventual completion, may never be known. One reason for this situation is the paucity of information left by Chadwick. Yellin wrote that the composer,

> Unlike those voluble composers of today whose explanations surpass their music in interest and in length, was content to let the music speak for itself. He dealt in effective and expressive sound rather than in highfalutin' concepts, was direct, clear and always practical.[1]

Nevertheless, what is known is interesting for a variety of reasons. First, not all of them were conceived as symphonic works; that is, at least two of them, the Second Symphony and *Symphonic Sketches,* were begun as single-movement works that stood alone. Chadwick did not begin them with the notion of creating multi-movement, cyclical compositions. That accounts for the stylistic dissimilarity between these two works and Chadwick's other symphonic compositions, most notably the First and Third Symphonies.

Second, it must be noted that Chadwick apparently worked fairly quickly; with the exception of his First Symphony (begun when he was a student) and the works not conceived as symphonic (each of which had a comparatively lengthy germination period), he was able to compose large works within about a year. Chadwick's speed produced mixed results; generally, the critics scorned the Third Symphony, even though it received a major prize at a respected competition, then chaired by Dvořák. The *Suite Symphonique* won a prize as well, but similarly suffered the critics' wrath. On the other hand, the *Sinfonietta* was well-received by most writers as a delightful and well-crafted work, but lacking in true symphonic depth.

Third, Chadwick dedicated his symphonic works to prominent musicians of his time, including Theodore Thomas (Third Symphony), Frederick Shepherd Converse (*Symphonic Sketches*), and Frederick Stock (*Suite Symphonique*). These dedications demonstrate Chadwick's collegiality and the extent to which he was involved with the most respected artists and musicians of his day.

AESTHETIC MODELS IN EUROPEAN SYMPHONIC TRADITION

Analysis of Chadwick's symphonic works has provided unexpected results. One might expect that, as a composer's skills are practiced, he would become more fluent in the art of symphonic composition. In Chadwick's case that is certainly true. Given Chadwick's rigorous Teutonic training, however, one might also expect that he would forge ahead, as his American predecessor John Knowles Paine did, to higher levels of technical artistry. It seems, however, that shortly after composing his Third Symphony, Chadwick abandoned the austere Germanic style of composition and turned to a lighter, more rhapsodic style, which he had first begun to explore in the second movement of the Second Symphony. Chadwick's new outlook on composition included more emphasis on melody, rhythm, and orchestration. This fundamental change in Chadwick's compositional values marks the beginning of a shift in American composition away from German influence to French.

In his article "Unity and Ensemble: Contrasting Ideals in Romantic Music," Brian Primmer discussed the differences between these national styles of composition that apply to Chadwick's abrupt change of approach. Primmer noted that German composers and critics placed a great deal of importance on counterpoint and the organic unfolding of a work. He stated that

> For them, organicism had to be a teleological experience: it had to have a purpose, and to move toward an end which had been implicit from the start.[2]

Comparing organic growth in music to Nature, Primmer continued,

> The lessons which Nature taught were those of slow development and growth. For her, Time was a continuum through which to unfold purposively . . . and her workings could be discovered as much in the distant past as in the immediate present or the longed-for future.[3]

Organicism played a minor role in Chadwick's compositional thinking, at least in his later works. The First Symphony displays some organic development, as do the Second and Third Symphonies. After these, however, organicism becomes noticeably less important, and counterpoint and traditional symphonic development are replaced by color, innovation, and contrast.

Chadwick's early years in Europe with the Duveneck Boys and his frequent vacations to France in his later life certainly had a good deal of impact on him. Commenting on Chadwick's 1879 summer in France, Yellin wrote,

> Considering the French and Italian orientation of his mature style . . . it may not be too extreme to suggest that the seeds of this taste were formed by the fleeting exposure to French culture during these magic months of creative growth.[4]

It has been mentioned that Chadwick had ample opportunity to study various French scores, if not to hear the works performed. We may surmise that Chadwick recognized as a key element of the French style what Primmer discovered to be a most important point in his discussion of "contrasting ideals." Primmer wrote that

> Once music generally had been conceived of as a language, the rational techniques of good dramatic writing might logically be applied to it. Of all such literary doctrines and dramatic techniques none was more important than that of *contrastes, oppositions, combinaisons, et effets*; and I do not think it is too much to claim that the deliberate collision of contrasts and oppositions, so deployed as to produce *amazing effects* [emphasis mine] through startlingly varied and unexpected combinations, remained the very foundation of Gallic music in the nineteenth century. Extended now beyond the operatic milieu to cover all branches of the musical art, and making full use of every subtlety of timbre and nuance which the times had to command, it was among the chief vehicles of musical Romanticism in the land.[5]

This idea of using astonishing effects and "every subtlety of timbre and nuance" had an impact on Chadwick, especially in the second movement of his Second Symphony, in *Symphonic Sketches* and *Suite Symphonique,* and to a lesser extent in the *Sinfonietta*. The effects that Chadwick used were diverse: pentatonicism or nearly pentatonic passages, "orientalism," prominent use of wind and percussion instruments, special instrumental techniques such as harmonics, employment of "ragged" and other syncopated rhythms, and even an occasional allusion to a folksong. While analysis has revealed that the First and Third Symphonies are built according to more traditional symphonic principles, by and large Chadwick's other symphonic works clearly exhibit the French-influenced traits Primmer identified above.

Further corroborating Chadwick's turn to Gallic influence is his use of descriptive titles in his works rather than the generic title "symphony." As Primmer noted, preambular titles, poems, and the like attached to musical works are characteristics of the French tradition.[6]

STYLISTIC AND STRUCTURAL TENDENCIES

Chadwick was content to work in traditional forms. Only rarely did he wander far from standard sonata forms in his first or fourth movements, the sole exceptions being the fourth movements of *Symphonic Sketches* and the *Suite Symphonique*. In the First Symphony (mvt. 1), *Symphonic Sketches* (mvt. 1), *Sinfonietta* (mvts. 1

and 4), *Suite Symphonique* (mvt. 1), the music proceeds from the tonic to the mediant rather than to the expected dominant. Although movement to the mediant is not highly unusual, it does indicate that Chadwick was attempting to move away from the most conventional aspect of sonata structure, the tonic-dominant contrast. Perhaps the composer did this because the tonic-dominant relationship had become obvious and predictable; in that event, movement to the mediant would seem more dramatic than movement to the dominant. The achievement of contrast in Chadwick's music relies upon the introduction of new themes and their development to a much greater extent than on harmonic development. This, of course, was a compositional trend that had occurred throughout the nineteenth century. The final movements of *Symphonic Sketches* and the *Suite Symphonique* are the ultimate expressions of Chadwick's departure from tradition. In the former, sonata form is completely abandoned in favor of a rondolike, five-part, multi-thematic movement that provides practically no harmonic drama at all. Chadwick is able to maintain the listeners' attention, however, by exploring various themes. In the latter, Chadwick employs sonata form, but the harmonic movement is decidedly nontraditional and does not heighten the sense of drama. The burden of creating drama and interest is placed upon the themes.

Another important stylistic hallmark of Chadwick's works is his employment of multi-sectional codas. In all of Chadwick's symphonic compositions, save his last two, *Sinfonietta* and *Suite Symphonique,* he used multi-sectional codas. In these structures, Chadwick was able to concentrate solely on the development of melodic material without regard to harmonic contrast; almost without exception, harmonic development had no role in this section of Chadwick's works. Thus, it would not be too much to say that the clearest manifestations of Chadwick's emphasis on thematic development in his sonata structures, not to mention his penchant for finalelike endings, are found in his multi-sectional codas. At the very least, Chadwick's codas, with their virtuosic, finalelike flair, reflect Primmer's statement above regarding the "amazing effects" produced by Chadwick's codas' extremely abrupt contrasts.

The inner movements of Chadwick's symphonic compositions are most often multi-sectional structures (usually in three or five parts) or brief sonata forms. The most obvious exception to this is the third movement of *Symphonic Sketches,* which is in sonata form but, at 500 measures, is hardly brief. While they exhibit little in the way of formal ingenuity, it was in these inner movements that Chadwick composed some of his most memorable passages. The second movement of the Second Symphony has already been mentioned for its importance, but several other inner movements should not be overlooked, including the third movement saltarello of the Third Symphony, the "Hobgoblin" movement of *Symphonic Sketches,* the second movement canzonetta of the *Sinfonietta,* and the ingenious third movement "Intermezzo and Humoreske" of the *Suite Symphonique.*

Consideration of the inner movements of these works leads to another observation, that Chadwick usually did not compose cyclic symphonic works. These compositions are not unified by traditional means. The First Symphony, the work one would most expect to be unified in this manner because it is one of the composer's earliest efforts, is not cyclic. Several movements in the Second and in the Third Symphonies share common material, but Chadwick employed this technique only rarely, and usually without subtlety. In his last three symphonic works Chadwick completely cast aside the interrelation of respective movements of his works in this manner.

CRITICAL RECEPTION

The critical reviews that Chadwick received for his symphonic works are valuable in a number of respects. First, they indicate the attention that the composer was able to garner throughout his career. While the reviews were not always favorable, the fact that he was afforded so much attention by some of the most important critics of the day shows the extent to which he was known and respected in the musical community. Second, the reviews clearly display the importance that the writers placed on the most urgent musical issues of their time, nationalism in American music and the forging of an American style. While the writing often falls into discussion of "spirit" and other musical intangibles, several critics discuss the technical aspects of the works with a great deal of competence. In fact, the astonishing use of technical jargon in some of the reviews not only gives the reader confidence in the judgment of the critic, but also offers an impressive indication of the high level of musical literacy of the concertgoing public. Third, in one of the most unexpected findings in this study, reviews of those performances conducted by the composer show the likelihood that Chadwick's inadequacy on the podium undermined the success of some of his works.

The review of the First Symphony was befitting of a young composer's first effort in the genre. The critic simply noted that it was well crafted, even imaginative in some respects, and finished with a few remarks of encouragement. Chadwick made a real impact on the genre, and a most favorable impression on the reviewers, beginning with his Second Symphony. Critics regularly noted the work's "spontaneity," the "lightness," and "the general lack of true seriousness," characteristics that would be a hallmark of his later style.[7] While the Second Symphony has been described in the musicological literature as a resounding success, this was not entirely the case. More than a few writers failed to find the work up to the standards they would expect either for a symphony or for a composer who, even at his young age, was already known and respected.

Although the Third Symphony was honored with a prestigious prize, it suffered by constant comparison to the popular Second Symphony, or, more precisely, the second movement of that work. Unlike the earlier symphony, the Third Symphony was viewed as a contrived, uninspired work. Several writers derisively noted the obvious stylistic debt that Chadwick owed to Brahms, but perhaps those charges were unfair; after all, most serious composers of that time were deeply affected by the German master. Of course, the symphony was not without those who thought it an impressive and important accomplishment. But given the fact that it was Chadwick's last true "symphony," it is possible that he took the negative reviews more seriously than the positive.

There can be little doubt that Chadwick's elimination of the title "symphony" in his last three symphonic works had a profound impact on their reception. Beginning with *Symphonic Sketches,* the tone of the reviews, along with the expectations of the reviewers, changed completely. Critics no longer occupied themselves with the internal workings of the respective compositions but were enthralled by the American spirit, the jolly tunes, the rambunctiousness, and the inspired orchestration they heard in these compositions. *Symphonic Sketches* was universally embraced for its verve and energy. The *Sinfonietta,* actually an attempt by Chadwick to compose in a more traditionally symphonic vein than he had in the *Symphonic Sketches,* was hailed for its cheerful nature and its "American-ness." The *Suite Symphonique,* also the winning entry in a prestigious competition, created a generally positive response from those who were not familiar with *Symphonic Sketches.* The *Suite* was also lauded for its positive outlook and its avoidance of the "strange scales and weird chords" so prevalent in contemporary composition. But those who were familiar with the earlier *Symphonic Sketches* considered the *Suite Symphonique* a failed attempt to recapture past glory.

Chadwick's success in the area of symphonic music began to wane noticeably after *Symphonic Sketches.* Part of the reason for this may simply have to do with the politics of performance in his day with regard to American composers. One Boston critic, in attendance at a special evening of music by Chadwick performed by the Boston Symphony Orchestra, wondered why Chadwick was being honored with a special night. He believed that, rather than being patronized with an evening dedicated to his music, Chadwick's works deserved to take their rightful place among the standard repertoire. He stated,

> To turn to last night's concert, it must at once be set down as a success. The wonder of it is, however, why such a concert should have been necessary. Why have Mr. Chadwick's best works not been produced elsewhere with sufficient frequency to make a concert of the character of last night's out of the question? There was an audience of good size and of enviable quality, that showed itself intensely interested, and, at times, highly enthusiastic. The approval of such people as were present at Jordan Hall yesterday evening demonstrates that Mr. Chadwick's best work is valuable. Why, then, is it not oftener performed?[8]

Another reason for Chadwick's lack of success is that, after about 1905, he was behind the times. The Third Symphony, well-crafted and cast in the Brahmsian/Dvořákian mold, was still acceptable in the early 1890s. *Symphonic Sketches,* a work not attacked on the grounds of technique, but embraced for its "spirit," was out of the ordinary and, therefore, also acceptable. But Chadwick's later symphonic works belonged to an older style of composition. Although the *Sinfonietta* was not without charm and the *Suite Symphonique* also had some inspired moments, by and large they were out of touch with the latest fashions. Whether or not the general audience felt this we cannot be sure; but the critics thought it true, and we may suppose that the younger generation of composers did also.

Henry T. Parker, writing of Chadwick's tone poem *Angel of Death* in 1919, noted that, like all of Chadwick's later works, including tone poems *Cleopatra* and *Aphrodite,* it was "willed and manufactured music of Mr. Chadwick's later, more sterile years."[9] This quote is particularly relevant to the present discussion because *Cleopatra* was completed in 1904, at approximately the same time as the *Sinfonietta* and well before the *Suite Symphonique*. In 1919, when Parker wrote his review, he was able to look back at Chadwick's career and judge that no works of great value were composed after *Symphonic Sketches,* a composition the critic admired tremendously. In his *Angel of Death* review, Parker continued,

> The rays of Mr. Chadwick's study lamp, not the heat of creative passion within, warm it. Has he, rich in the laurels of his prime, with a voice on occasion more American than that of any other symphonic composer, need to set down so many pages of barren measures that in his sixties he may still "keep on"?[10]

One of the most sobering accounts of the legacy of Chadwick's symphonic music was written in the composer's death notice in the *New York Times* on April 5, 1931. The section of the notice concerning Chadwick's compositions read as follows:

> Among his best known compositions have been "Viking Voyage" for men's voices; the overture "Melpomene," the comic opera "Tabasco," the overture "The Miller's Daughter," "The Pilgrim's Hymn," and the "Columbian Ode," written for the World's Fair of 1893, and "Phoenix Expirans," considered his finest choral work. He also wrote much church music.[11]

There is absolutely no mention of his work in symphonic music in this account of Chadwick's life. Two prizewinning symphonic compositions (Third Symphony and *Suite Symphonique*) and at least two popular and well-known works (Second Symphony and *Symphonic Sketches*) were completely overlooked by the writer.

If the mention of Chadwick's symphonic works was sparse, the acclaim he received for his entire oeuvre upon his passing was enviable. Olin Downes wrote a lengthy article about the composer just after his death on April 4, 1931. But his most stirring remembrance of Chadwick came in August of that year, when Downes wrote,

> George Whitefield Chadwick died the 4th of last April, at the age of 77, a very distinguished musician and on the whole the greatest American composer of his age and generation. He was a symphonist and a composer in nearly all the larger forms. In a certain number of his works he struck a personal and genuinely American note, and his technical equipment was such as to command the highest respect on both sides of the Atlantic. Mr. Chadwick came of a New England generation with "background" and culture. He cherished the highest ideals of his art. He had studied with Reinecke in Leipzig and with Rheinberger in Munich. He was what the Westerner called a gentleman and a scholar, and a creative musician of racy wit and temperament besides. After MacDowell, Chadwick did the most to give the American composer international standing, and his range of expression was wider than MacDowell's, if his feeling was not so mystical and poetic.[12]

It cannot be said that these six compositions by Chadwick greatly impacted either the symphonic genre or the course of music in America. By the end of the First World War, Chadwick's efforts in symphonic composition had been forgotten, and new ideas had captured the imaginations of the younger generation of composers. Only now, with the renewed interest in American music, is orchestral music composed before World War I being explored, studied, discussed, and recorded. Taken as a whole, however, Chadwick's symphonic works represent a high point in American composition; not only do these works explore new possibilities of a uniquely American style of composition, but they are well-crafted, witty, and ingenious, and were understood and appreciated, if not universally admired, in their own time.

NOTES

NOTES TO CHAPTER 1

1. Victor Fell Yellin, *Chadwick, Yankee Composer* (Washington, D.C.: Smithsonian Institution Press, 1990), 12.
2. H. Wiley Hitchcock and Stanley Sadie, eds. *The New Grove Dictionary of American Music* (London: Macmillan, 1986), s.v. "Chadwick, George Whitefield," by Victor Fell Yellin and Stephen Ledbetter.
3. Yellin, *Chadwick, Yankee Composer,* 22.
4. Ibid., 27.
5. Victor Fell Yellin, "Chadwick, American Musical Realist," *Musical Quarterly,* 61 (1975): 82.
6. Ibid., 79.
7. Yellin, *Chadwick, Yankee Composer,* 35.
8. E. Douglas Bomberger, "The German Musical Training of American Students, 1850–1900," (Ph.D. diss., University of Maryland, 1991), 136.
9. Yellin, *Chadwick, Yankee Composer,* 39.
10. Ibid., 43.
11. Ibid., 44.
12. Ibid., 43.
13. Ibid., 76.
14. Ibid., 68–69.
15. Ibid.
16. Ibid., 72.
17. W.S.B. Mathews, "The American Composer and American Concert Programs," *The Musician* 8/6 (June 1903): 204.
18. Yellin, *Chadwick, Yankee Composer,* 80–81.
19. Hitchcock and Sadie, *American Music,* 385.
20. *Boston Evening Transcript,* November 17, 1919, 13.

NOTES TO CHAPTER 2

1. Nicholas E. Tawa, *The Coming of Age of American Art Music* (Westport, Conn.: Greenwood, 1991), 89–93.

2. Henry F. Gilbert, "The American Composer," *Musical Quarterly* 1/1 (1915): 171.
3. Tawa, *Coming of Age,* 59.

NOTES TO CHAPTER 3

1. *The Sunday Herald* (Boston), February 19, 1882.
2. *Dwight's Journal of Music,* January 15, 1881, 15.
3. Ibid., December 20, 1879, 205.
4. Gilbert Chase, *America's Music* (Urbana, Ill.: University of Illinois Press, 1987), 341.
5. William Arlie Everett, "The Symphonies of John Knowles Paine," (Master's thesis, Southern Methodist University, 1986), 12.
6. Nicholas E. Tawa, *The Coming of Age of American Art Music* (Westport, Conn.: Greenwood, 1991), 2.
7. George Whitefield Chadwick, "American Composers," in *History of American Music,* ed. W. L. Hubbard (Toledo: Irving Squire, 1908), 2.
8. Victor Fell Yellin, *Chadwick, Yankee Composer* (Washington, D.C.: Smithsonian Institution Press, 1990), 30.
9. *Boston Evening Transcript,* February 24, 1882, 30.
10. Ibid.

NOTES TO CHAPTER 4

1. Victor Fell Yellin, *Chadwick, Yankee Composer* (Washington, D.C.: Smithsonian Institution Press, 1990), 93.
2. Steven Ledbetter, "George W. Chadwick: A Sourcebook" MS, 1983 [photocopy], Spaulding Library of the New England Conservatory of Music (Boston), 94.
3. *Boston Evening Transcript,* January 15, 1883, 1.
4. David Beveridge, "Sophisticated Primitivism: The Significance of Primitivism in Dvořák's American Quartet," *Current Musicology* 24 (1977): 25.
5. Ibid., 26.
6. Ibid., 30.
7. *Boston Evening Transcript,* March 10, 1884, 1.
8. Ibid., December 13, 1886, 1.
9. Ibid.
10. Ibid.
11. *Boston Post,* December 13, 1886.

12. Ibid.
13. Ibid.
14. Ibid.
15. Ibid.
16. *Boston Herald,* December 12, 1886.
17. Ibid.
18. Ibid.
19. Ibid.
20. Unidentified clipping, Allen A. Brown Collection, Boston Public Library, dated December 11, 1886.
21. Ibid.
22. Ibid.
23. Unidentified clipping, Allen A. Brown Collection, Boston Public Library, n.d.
24. Ibid.
25. Ibid.
26. W.S.B. Mathews, "Music at the Fair," *Music* 4 (1893): 226.
27. H. Wiley Hitchcock and Stanley Sadie, eds. *The New Grove Dictionary of American Music* (London: Macmillan, 1986), s.v. "Mathews, W.S.B.," by Robert W. Groves.
28. Unidentified clipping, Allen A. Brown Collection, Boston Public Library, n.d.
29. Ibid.
30. Ibid.

NOTES TO CHAPTER 5

1. Victor Fell Yellin, *Chadwick, Yankee Composer* (Washington, D.C.: Smithsonian Institution Press, 1990), 96.
2. *American Art Journal,* April 21, 1894, 25.
3. M. A. DeWolfe Howe, *The Boston Symphony Orchestra 1881–1931* (Cambridge, Mass.: Riverside, 1931), 189.
4. Ibid., 195
5. *Boston Evening Transcript,* October 22, 1894, 4.
6. Ibid.
7. Ibid.
8. Ibid.
9. *New York Musical Courier,* October 19, 1894.
10. Ibid.
11. Ibid.
12. Ibid.
13. Ibid.

14. Unidentified clipping, Allen A. Brown Collection, Boston Public Library, n.d.
15. Ibid.
16. Ibid.
17. Ibid.
18. Unidentified clipping, Allen A. Brown Collection, Boston Public Library, n.d.
19. Ibid.
20. Ibid.
21. Unidentified clipping, Allen A. Brown Collection, Boston Public Library, dated [by hand] 1896.
22. Unidentified clipping, Allen A. Brown Collection, Boston Public Library, n.d.
23. *Boston Globe,* December 29, 1905.
24. Ibid.

NOTES TO CHAPTER 6

1. Victor Fell Yellin, *Chadwick, Yankee Composer* (Washington, D.C.: Smithsonian Institution Press, 1990), 112.
2. Steven Ledbetter, "George W. Chadwick: A Sourcebook" MS, 1983 [photocopy], Spaulding Library of the New England Conservatory of Music (Boston), 100.

NOTES TO CHAPTER 7

1. Steven Ledbetter, "George W. Chadwick: A Sourcebook" MS, 1983 [photocopy], Spaulding Library of the New England Conservatory of Music (Boston), 89.
2. Ibid., 84.
3. Victor Fell Yellin, *Chadwick, Yankee Composer* (Washington, D.C.: Smithsonian Institution Press, 1990), 113.
4. Ibid., 119.
5. Victor Fell Yellin, "Chadwick, American Musical Realist," *Musical Quarterly,* 61 (1975): 77–97.
6. Ibid., 89–90.
7. Ibid., 89.
8. Ibid.
9. Yellin, *Chadwick, Yankee Composer,* 113.

10. David Beveridge, "Sophisticated Primitivism: The Significance of Primitivism in Dvořák's American Quartet," *Current Musicology* 24 (1977), 26.
11. *Boston Herald,* November 22, 1904.
12. Unidentified clipping, Allen A. Brown Collection, Boston Public Library (ca. November 22, 1904).
13. Ibid.
14. Ibid.
15. Unidentified clipping, Allen A. Brown Collection, Boston Public Library, n.d.
16. Ibid.
17. *Boston Evening Transcript,* February 10, 1908.
18. Ibid.
19. Ibid.
20. Ibid.
21. Ibid.
22. Ibid.
23. *Boston Globe,* February 9, 1908.
24. *Boston Herald,* March 23, 1918.
25. Ibid.
26. Ibid.
27. Ibid.

NOTES TO CHAPTER 8

1. M. A. DeWolfe Howe, *The Boston Symphony Orchestra, 1881–1931* (Cambridge, Mass.: Riverside, 1931), 188.
2. Ibid., 187.
3. *Boston Evening Transcript,* November 22, 1904, 15.
4. *Boston Herald,* November 22, 1904.
5. Ibid.
6. Unidentified clipping, Allen A. Brown Collection, Boston Public Library, n.d.
7. *New York Sun,* January 16, 1910.
8. *Boston Journal,* February 12, 1910.
9. *Boston Post,* February 12, 1910.
10. Ibid.
11. *Boston Monitor,* February 14, 1910.
12. *Boston Evening Transcript,* February 12, 1910.
13. Ibid.
14. *New York Sun,* January 3, 1910.
15. Ibid.
16. Ibid.

NOTES TO CHAPTER 9

1. Steven Ledbetter, "George W. Chadwick: A Sourcebook" MS, 1983 [photocopy], Spaulding Library of the New England Conservatory of Music (Boston), 85.
2. *Philadelphia Inquirer,* March 30, 1911, 2.
3. *Evening Bulletin* (Philadelphia), March 30, 1911, 4.
4. *Boston Evening Transcript,* April 14, 1911.
5. Theodore Baker, *Baker's Biographical Dictionary of Musicians,* 6th edition rev. by Nicholas Slonimsky (New York: G. Schirmer, 1978), 1721.
6. *Boston Evening Transcript,* April 14, 1911.
7. *New York Times,* February 3, 1912.
8. Ibid.
9. Unidentified clipping, Allen A. Brown Collection, Boston Public Library, n.d.
10. Ibid.
11. Ibid.
12. Ibid.

NOTES TO CHAPTER 10

1. Personal letter to the author, September 5, 1990.
2. Brian Primmer, "Unity and Ensemble: Contrasting Ideals in Romantic Music," *19th-Century Music* 6/2 (Fall 1982), 106.
3. Ibid.
4. Victor Fell Yellin, *Chadwick, Yankee Composer* (Washington, D.C.: Smithsonian Institution Press, 1990), 37.
5. Primmer, "Unity and Ensemble," 110.
6. Ibid., 117.
7. *Boston Evening Transcript,* December 13, 1886.
8. Ibid., November 22, 1904.
9. Ibid., November 17, 1919.
10. Ibid.
11. *New York Times,* April 5, 1931.
12. Ibid., August 9, 1931.

APPENDIX I

THE COMPLETE WORKS OF GEORGE WHITEFIELD CHADWICK

EXPLANATORY NOTE

This listing includes:
title
genre and/or key and/or opus number (for large works)
date of composition; year and location of premiere (for large works)
place and date of publication (if published)
shortened publisher reference

In those instances in which a premiere has not yet occurred or is unknown, only the date of composition is listed. If neither the premiere date nor year of composition is known, such is stated. Stage and vocal works include librettists and/or translators where possible. In most cases, premiere dates of smaller works have not been recorded.

KEY TO PUBLISHERS

C. C. Birchard (Boston), Boston Music Company (Boston), John Church (Cincinnati), Oliver Ditson (Boston), H. W. Gray (New York), T. B. Harms (New York), J. B. Millet (New York), Novello (London), L. Prang (Boston), G. Schirmer (New York), Arthur P. Schmidt (Boston), Charles Scribner (New York), Silver Burdett (Boston), B. F. Wood (Boston).

Works list based on Ledbetter (1983).

A. *INSTRUMENTAL MUSIC*

1. *Orchestral Music*

Rip Van Winkle, overture (1879 [rev. 1920]; 1879, Leipzig), Boston 1930, Birchard

Schön München, waltz (1880; 1881, Boston), Ms.

Symphony No. 1 C op. 5 (1881; 1882, Boston), Ms.

Andante G (1882; 1882, Boston), Ms.

Thalia, overture (1882; 1883, Boston), Ms.

Symphony No. 2 B^b (1883–1885; Mvt. II, 1884; complete 1886, Boston), Boston 1930, Schmidt

The Miller's Daughter, orchestral song (for baritone) and overture (1886; 1887, San Francisco), Ms.

Melpomene, dramatic overture (1887; 1887, Boston), Ms.

A Pastoral Prelude (1890; 1892, Boston), Ms.

Serenade F (1890), Ms.

Symphony No. 3 F (1893–1894; 1894, Boston), Boston 1896, Schmidt

Tabasco March for band or orchestra (1894; 1894, Boston), Boston 1894, Wood (piano arrangement)

Adonais, overture (1899; 1900, Boston), Ms.

Euterpe, overture (1903; 1904, Boston), New York 1906, Schirmer

Cleopatra, symphonic poem (1904; 1904, Worcester, Mass.), Ms.

Sinfonietta D (1904; 1904, Boston), New York 1906, Schirmer

Theme, Variations, and Fugue (with organ) (1908; 1908, Boston), Boston 1923, Boston Music Company (organ arrangement)

Everywoman Waltz (1909), Ms.

Suite Symphonique E^b (1905–1909; 1911, Philadelphia) Boston 1911, Schmidt

Aphrodite, symphonic fantasy (1910–1911; 1912, Norfolk, Conn.), Ms.

Tam O'Shanter, symphonic ballad (1914–1915; 1915, Norfolk, Conn.), Boston 1917, Boston Music Company

Angel of Death, symphonic poem (1917–1918; 1919, New York), Ms.

Jericho March (1919?), Ms.

Elegy (1920), Ms.

Anniversary Overture (1922?; 1922, Norfolk, Conn.), Ms.

Tre Pezzi (1923), Ms.

2. *Chamber Music*

String Quartet No. 1 g op. 1 (1878; 1878, Leipzig), Ms.

String Quartet No. 2 C op. 2 (1878; 1879, Leipzig), Ms.

String Quartet No. 3 D (1885?; 1887, Boston), Ms.

Quintet E^b for piano, 2 violins, viola and cello (1887; 1888, Boston), Boston 1911, Schmidt

String Quartet No. 4 e (1896; 1896, Boston), New York 1902, Schirmer (parts only)

String Quartet No. 5 d (1898; 1901, Boston), Ms.

Romanze for cello and piano (1911), Boston 1911, Schmidt

Easter Morn for violin or cello and piano (1914?), Boston 1914, Schmidt

Fanfare for 3 trumpets, 3 trombones and timpani (1925; 1925, Boston), Ms.

3. *Piano Music*

Six Characteristic Pieces op. 7 (unknown), Boston 1882, Schmidt

Two Caprices C g (unknown), Boston 1888, Schmidt

Drei Walzer f E♭ A♭ (unknown), Boston 1890, Schmidt

Melpomene, (4 hands) (1887), Boston 1891, Schmidt

Chanson orientale (unknown), New York 1895, Millet

Nocturne (unknown), New York 1895, Millet

Ten Little Tunes for Ten Little Fingers (unknown), Boston 1903, Wood

Five Pieces (unknown), New York 1905, Schirmer

Aphrodite, (2 pianos) (1910), Ms.

Diddle Diddle Dumpling (unknown), Boston 1928, New England Conservatory of Music

Ye Robin (unknown), Boston 1928, New England Conservatory of Music

The Footlight Fairy (unknown), Ms.

Novelette (unknown), Ms.

Prelude and Fugue (a la hornpipe) G (unknown), Ms. (copy)

Prelude and Fugue a (unknown), Ms. (copy)

Prelude and Fugue c (unknown), Ms.

4. *Organ Music*

Ten Canonic Studies op. 12 (unknown), Boston 1885, Schmidt

Progressive Pedal Studies (unknown), Boston 1890, Schmidt

Three Compositions (unknown), Boston 1890, Schmidt

Pastorale (unknown), New York 1895, Millet

Requiem D^b (1895), New York 1896, Millet

Canzonetta G (unknown), New York 1896, Millet

Introduction and Theme E^b (unknown), New York 1896, Millet

Elegy [in memoriam Horatio Parker] (unknown), Boston 1920, Boston Music Company

Suite in Variation Form (unknown), New York 1923, Gray

In Tadaussac Church (1735) (unknown), New York 1926, Gray

B. *STAGE WORKS*

The Peer and the Pauper (R. Grant), comic operetta in 2 acts (1884), Ms.

A Quiet Lodging (A. Bates), operetta in 2 acts (1892; 1892, Boston), Ms. [Lost except No. 5]

Tabasco (R. A. Barnet), burlesque opera in 2 acts (1893–1894; 1894 Boston), Boston 1894, Wood

Judith (W. C. Langdon), lyric drama in 3 acts (1899–1900; 1901 Worcester, Mass.), New York 1901, Schirmer

Everywoman (W. Browne), incidental music in 5 acts (1910; 1911 Hartford, Conn.), New York 1911, T. B. Harms

The Padrone (D. Stevens), opera in 2 acts (1912–1913), Ms.

Love's Sacrifice (D. Stevens), pastoral opera in 1 act (1916–1917; 1923 Chicago), Boston 1917, Birchard.

C. *CHORAL MUSIC*

1. *With Orchestra*

The Viking's Last Voyage (S. Baxter) for baritone and men's chorus (1881; 1881 Boston), Boston 1881, Schmidt

The Song of the Viking (Craigin) for men's chorus (1882 [orchestrated 1914]; 1886 Boston), Boston 1882, Schmidt [piano-vocal score only]

Dedication Ode op. 15 (H. B. Carpenter), for SATB and mixed chorus (1883; 1883 Boston), Boston 1886, Schmidt [piano-vocal score only]

Lovely Rosabelle (Scott) for soprano, tenor and mixed chorus (1889; 1889 Boston), Boston 1889, Schmidt [piano-vocal score only]

Lullaby (unknown) for women's chorus (unknown) Boston 1899, Schmidt [piano-vocal score only]

The Pilgrims (F. D. Hemans) for mixed chorus (1890; 1891 Boston), Boston 1890, Schmidt [piano-vocal score only]

Phoenix Expirans (anonymous) for SATB and mixed chorus (1891; 1892 Springfield, Mass.), Boston 1892, Schmidt [piano-vocal score only]

Ode (H. Monroe) for soprano, tenor, and mixed chorus (1892; 1892 Chicago), Cincinnati 1892, Church [piano-vocal score only]

The Lily Nymph (A. Bates) for soprano, tenor, baritone, and bass and mixed chorus (1895; 1895 New York), Boston 1895, Schmidt [piano-vocal score only]

Ecce jam noctis (St. Gregory; trans. Isabella Parker) for men's chorus (1897; 1897 New Haven, Conn.), Boston 1897, Schmidt [piano-vocal score]

Noel (I. M. Chadwick, et al.) for SATB and mixed chorus (1908; 1909 Norfolk, Conn.), New York 1909, Gray [piano-vocal score only]

Elfin Song (J. R. Drake) for women's chorus (1913 [orch. arr. of song previously published]), Boston 1910, Schmidt [piano-vocal score only]

Silently Swaying on the Water's Quiet Breast (V. von Scheffel; trans. Isabella Parker) for women's chorus (1916?), Boston 1916, Ditson [piano-vocal score only]

Jehovah Reigns in Majesty (Ps. 99) for men's chorus and organ (1916?), Boston 1916, Ditson [piano-vocal score only]

Land of Our Hearts (J. H. Ingam) for mixed chorus (1917; 1918 Norfolk, Conn.), Cincinnati 1918, Church [piano-vocal score only]

These to the Front (M. A. DeWolfe Howe) for men's chorus (1918), Boston 1918, Ditson [piano-vocal score only]

The Fighting Men (M. A. DeWolfe Howe) for unison voices (1918?) Boston 1918, Birchard [piano-vocal score only]

Joshua (R. D. Ware) for men's chorus (1919?), Boston 1919, Ditson [piano-vocal score only]

Mexican Serenade (A. Guiterman) for mixed chorus (1921?), Boston 1921, Silver Burdett [piano-vocal score only]

Fathers of the Free (E. E. Brown) for mixed chorus (1927?), New York 1927, Gray [piano-vocal score only]

Commemoration Ode (J. R. Lowell) for mixed chorus (1928?), Boston 1928, Ditson [piano-vocal score only]

2. *With Piano*

The Song of the Viking (Craigin) for men's chorus (1881–1882?), Boston 1882, Schmidt

Spring Song op. 9 (anonymous) for women's chorus, Boston 1882, Schmidt

Lullaby (unknown) for women's chorus, Boston 1889, Schmidt

Four Songs of Brittany (A. Bates) for women's chorus, Boston 1890, Schmidt

Three Choruses (Meleager) for women's chorus, New York 1904, Schirmer

Elfin Song (Joseph R. Drake) for women's chorus, Boston 1910, Schmidt

In a China Shop (G. C. Hellman) for women's chorus, Boston 1910, Schmidt

Miss Nancy's Gown (Zitella Cooke) for women's chorus, Boston 1910, Schmidt

Inconstancy (Shakespeare) for mixed chorus, women's chorus, or men's chorus [piano ad lib.], Boston 1910, Schmidt

It Was a Lover and His Lass (Shakespeare), for men's chorus or women's chorus [piano ad lib.], Boston 1910, Schmidt

The Spring Beauties (Helen Gray Cone) for women's chorus, Boston 1911, Schmidt

Noble's Traditions (Robert W. Rivers) for children's chorus, Boston 1913, published privately

Hail Us Doctors of Song (John Koren) for men's chorus, Boston 1914, The Sangerfest

Silently Swaying on the Water's Quiet Breast (V. von Scheffel; trans. Isabella Parker) for women's chorus, Boston 1916, Ditson

The Bluebells of New England (Thomas Bailey Aldrich) for women's chorus, Boston 1917, Ditson

Dolly (Auston Dobson) for women's chorus, Boston 1917, Ditson

The Fighting Men (M. A. DeWolfe Howe) for unison chorus, Boston 1918, Birchard

June (Justin H. Smith) for women's chorus, Boston 1918, Ditson

These to the Front (M. A. DeWolfe Howe) for men's chorus, Boston 1918, Ditson

Joshua (R. D. Ware) for men's chorus, Boston 1919, Ditson

Buie Annajohn (Bliss Carman) for mixed chorus, Boston 1923, Silver Burdett

Caravan Song (Alfred H. Hyatt) for mixed chorus, Boston 1923, Silver Burdett

Chorus of Pilgrim Women (Josephine P. Peabody) for women's chorus, Boston 1923, Silver Burdett

Deep in the Soul of a Rose (Alfred H. Hyatt) for women's chorus, Boston 1923, Silver Burdett

The Immortal or Spring Song (Cale Young Rice) for mixed chorus, Boston 1923, Birchard

Little Lac Grenie (William H. Drummond) for mixed chorus, Boston 1923, Silver Burdett

Mexican Serenade (Arthur Guiterman) for mixed chorus, Boston 1923, Silver Burdett

Mister Moon (Bliss Carman) for women's chorus, Boston 1923, Silver Burdett

A Christmas Greeting (unknown) for mixed chorus, Boston [?] 1925, published privately

A Ballad of Trees and the Master (piano or organ) (Sidney Lanier) for mixed chorus, Boston 1929, Ditson

Holiday Songs (O. W. Holmes [no. 1], R. W. Emerson [no. 2], S. Baring-Gould [no. 3], C. S. Pratt [no. 4], F. D. Sherman [no. 5], G. E. Troutlock [no. 6], C. Y. Rice [no. 8], M. B. Edwards [no. 9], G. F. Norton [no. 10]) for mixed chorus, Boston 1928, Ditson [piano ad lib. nos. 1, 3, 6, and 7]

Saint Botolph (Arthur Macy) for men's chorus, Boston 1929, Ditson.

3. *With Organ*

Three Sacred Anthems op. 6 (anonymous) for mixed chorus, Boston 1882, Schmidt.

Three Sacred Quartets op. 13 (Ps. 42 [no. 1], Bayard Taylor [no. 3]) for mixed chorus, Boston 1885, Schmidt

Abide with Me (unknown) for soprano, alto and tenor, Boston 1888, Schmidt

O Cease, My Wandering Soul (unknown) for soprano, alto, and bass, Boston 1888, Schmidt

O Day of Rest (unknown) for alto, tenor, and bass, Boston 1888, Schmidt

God Be Merciful (unknown) for mixed chorus, Boston 1890, Schmidt

The Beatitudes (unknown) for mixed chorus, Boston 1895, Schmidt

Jubilate in B^{b} (Ps. 100) for mixed chorus, Boston 1895, Schmidt

Lord of All Power and Might (unknown) for mixed chorus, Boston 1895, Schmidt

Peace and Light (unknown) for mixed chorus, Boston 1895, Schmidt

Sentences and Responses (unknown) for mixed chorus, Boston 1895, Schmidt

O Holy Child of Bethlehem (Phillips Brooks) for alto and mixed chorus, Boston 1896, Schmidt

Shout, Ye High Heavens (Plaudite Coeli [trans. John Lord Hayes]) for mixed chorus, Boston 1897, Schmidt

Hark! Hark My Soul (W. F. Faber) for alto and mixed chorus, New York 1903, Schirmer

Morn's Roseate Hues (unknown) for alto, bass, and mixed chorus (piano or organ), London 1903, Novello

Two Anthems (unknown) for mixed chorus, New York 1904, Schirmer

Savior, Again to Thy Dear Name (John Ellerton) for mixed chorus (piano or organ), London 1904, Novello

Sun of My Soul (John Keble) for tenor and mixed chorus, London 1904, Novello

Jehovah Reigns in Majesty (Ps. 99) for men's chorus and brass sextet, Boston 1916, Ditson.

4. *A Capella*

A. *For Mixed Chorus*

The Brightest and the Best (R. Heber), Boston 1888, Schmidt

There Were Shepherds, (unknown), Boston 1888, Schmidt

Thou Sendest Sun and Rain, (unknown), Boston 1889, Schmidt

Art Thou Weary?, (unknown), Boston 1890, Schmidt

Behold the Works of the Lord, (unknown), Boston 1891, Schmidt

Come Hither, Ye Faithful, (unknown), Boston 1891, Schmidt

Saviour, Like a Shepherd, (unknown), Boston 1891, Schmidt

While Thee I Seek, (unknown), Boston 1891, Schmidt

Awake Up My Glory, (unknown), Boston 1895, Schmidt

Thou Who Art Divine (adapted by O. B. Brown), Boston 1895, Schmidt

Welcome Happy Morn, (unknown), Boston 1895, Schmidt

When the Lord of Love Was Here (based on a hymn tune by Armstrong), Boston 1895, Schmidt

While Shepherds Watched, (unknown), Boston 1899, Schmidt

A Madrigal for Christmas (Chadwick?), Boston [?] ca. 1926, published privately

B. *For Women's Chorus*

Two Four-Part Choruses (G. da Todi [no. 1], Arthur Macy [no. 2]), New York 1902, Schirmer

Two Four-Part Choruses (J. C. Grant [no. 1], S. M. Peck [no. 2]), New York 1903, Schirmer

Mary's Lullaby (Cora A. Matson Dolson) [piano ad lib.], New York 1910, Schirmer

C. *For Children's Chorus*

Stormy Evening (Robert Louis Stevenson), Boston 1901, Birchard

Busy Lark (Chaucer), Boston 1912, Birchard

The Lamb (William Blake), Boston 1914, Birchard

Sons of Herman (J. L. Sanford), Boston 1914, Ditson

Here Comes the Flat (Arthur Macy), Boston 1918, Birchard

D. *For Men's Chorus*

Margarita (Scheffel) (1881), Boston 1881, Schmidt

Reiterlied (Trooper's Song) (1881), Boston 1881, Schmidt

Four Partsongs (John Leslie Breck [nos. 1–2], Arlo Bates [nos. 3–4]), Boston 1886, Schmidt

Jabberwocky (Lewis Carroll), Boston 1886, Schmidt

Three Part-songs (Walt Whitman [no. 1], Thackeray [no. 2], Thomas Heywood [no. 3, piano ad lib.]), Boston 1910, Schmidt

D. *SOLO SONGS*

1. *With Orchestra*

Lochinvar (Scott) for baritone (1896; 1896 Springfield, Mass.), Boston 1896, Schmidt (piano/vocal score)

A Ballad of Trees and the Master (S. Lanier) for low or medium voice (1899?), Ms.

Aghadoe (J. Todhunter) for alto (1910), Boston 1911, Schmidt (piano/vocal score)

The Curfew (Longfellow) for low or medium voice (1914?; 1924 Boston), Ms.

The Voice of Philomel (Stevens) for low or medium voice (1914?; 1924 Boston), Ms.

Joshua (Ware) for medium voice (1919?), Ms.

Drakes Drum (H. Newbold) for low or medium voice (1920?; 1924 Boston), Ms.

Pirate Song (A. Conan Doyle) for baritone (1920?), Ms.

2. *With Piano or Organ*

Three Songs by J. [*sic*] W. Chadwick (P. W. Lyall [no. 3 only]), Boston 1881, Ditson

The Miller's Daughter (Tennyson), Boston, 1881; Schmidt

Three Love Songs for baritone, op. 8 (A. Bates), Boston 1882, Schmidt

Three Little Songs, op. 11 (B. Cornwall [no. 1], Heine [no. 3]), Boston 1883, Schmidt

Six Songs (A. Bates [no. 1], N. MacIntosh [no. 2], Breck [no. 3], O. Leighton [no. 5]), Boston 1885, Schmidt

King Death (unknown), Boston 1885, Schmidt

The Sea King (Cornwall), Boston 1885, Schmidt

Two Songs (T. B. Aldrich), Boston 1886, Schmidt

The Mill (Mulock), Boston 1886, Schmidt

Allah (Longfellow), Boston 1887, Schmidt

The Lament (Egyptian song from "Ben Hur") (L. Wallace), Boston 1887, Schmidt

The Lily (A. Salvini; trans. by T. R. Sullivan), Boston 1887, Schmidt

Three Sacred Songs (H. H. Milman [no. 1], F. Baker [no. 2]), Boston 1887, Schmidt

Baby's Lullaby Book (C. S. Pratt), Boston 1888, Prang

Green Grows the Willow (H. Aide), Boston 1888, Schmidt

Sorais' Song (H. Rider Haggard), Boston 1888, Schmidt

The Brightest and the Best (unknown), Boston 1888, Schmidt

Three Ballads (A. Rives [no. 1], E. Breck [no. 3]), Boston 1889, Schmidt

Bedouin Love Song (I. S. Taylor), Boston 1890, Schmidt

Songs of Brittany (A. Bates), Boston 1890, Schmidt

A Flower Cycle (A. Bates), Boston 1890, Schmidt (reprinted in S. Ledbetter, *George W. Chadwick: Songs to Poems by Arlo Bates,* New York 1980, Da Capo)

Hail, All Hail the Glorious Morn (I. S. Taylor), Boston 1892, Schmidt

He Maketh War to Cease (unknown), Boston 1892, Schmidt

There Is a River (unknown), Boston 1892, Schmidt

Two Folk Songs (C. Rosetti [no. 2]), Boston 1892, Schmidt

Armenian Lullaby (E. Field), New York, 1896, Scribner

Kissing Time (E. Field), New York 1896, Scribner

Lyrics from "Told in the Gate" (A. Bates), Boston 1897, Schmidt (reprinted in S. Ledbetter, *George W. Chadwick: Songs to Poems by Arlo Bates,* New York 1980, Da Capo).

Farewell to the Farm (Stevenson), New York 1898, Scribner

I Have Not Forgotten (W. M. Chauvenet), Cincinnati 1898, Church

The Land of Counterpane (Stevenson), New York 1898, Scribner

Since My Love's Eyes (W. M. Chauvenet), Cincinnati 1898, Church

A Ballad of Trees and the Master (S. Lanier), Boston 1899, Ditson

Faith (Macy), Cincinnati 1899, Church

The Good Samaritan, with violin obbligato (J. Montgomery), Cincinnati 1900, Church

Six Songs (Macy [nos. 1–3, 5–6], W. M. Chauvenet [no. 4]), New York 1902, Schirmer

Three Songs for mezzo or baritone (W. M. Chauvenet [nos. 1 and 2], Macy [no. 3]), New York 1902, Schirmer

Saint Botolph (Macy), Boston 1902, Wood

Hark! Hark, My Soul (F. W. Faber), New York 1903, Schirmer

Four Irish Songs (Thackeray [no. 1], W. Maginn [no. 2], A. Moor [no. 3], R. W. Chambers [no. 4]), Boston 1910, Schmidt

Five Songs (B. Lytton [no. 1], J. Thomson [no. 2–3], Rossetti [no. 4], Sullivan [no. 5]), Boston 1910, Schmidt

Five Songs (Stevens), New York, 1914, Schirmer

The Curfew (Longfellow), Boston 1914, Schmidt

The Daughter of Mendoza (M. B. Lamar), Boston 1914, Schmidt

Fulfillment (Stevens), Boston 1914, Schmidt

Periwinkle Bay (Stevens), Boston 1914, Schmidt

That Golden Hour (Stevens), Boston 1914, Schmidt

Yesterday (Stevens), Boston 1914, Schmidt

The Fighting Men (Howe), Boston 1918, Birchard

Joshua (Ware), Boston 1920, Ditson

Three Nautical Songs (Ware [no. 1], Newbold [no. 2], A. Conan Doyle [no. 3]), Boston 1920, Ditson

A Christmas Limerick (Chadwick?), Boston [?] 1927, published privately

If I Were You (Hirsch?), [Recorded but no published copy or Ms. located]

Ladybird (Southey?), [Recorded but no published copy or Ms. located]

The Morning Glory (Foresman?), [Recorded but no published copy or Ms. located]

Time Enough (Braley?), [Recorded but no published copy or Ms. located]

APPENDIX II

SELECTED PERFORMANCES OF THE SYMPHONIC WORKS OF GEORGE WHITEFIELD CHADWICK

Under each heading the following information is provided: name of musical organization; date of performance(s) (month/day/year); name of conductor; section of composition performed. Premiere performances of complete works are also indicated.

SYMPHONY NO. 1

Harvard Musical Association (Boston)

02/23/1882	G. W. Chadwick	Complete (Premiere)

SYMPHONY NO. 2

Apollo Club (Boston)

04/29/1885	G. W. Chadwick	Mvt. 1 only
05/04/1885	G. W. Chadwick	Mvt. 1 only

Boston Symphony Orchestra

03/07-08/1884	George Henschel	Mvt. 2 only
12/10-11/1886	G. W. Chadwick	Complete (Premiere)
02/06-07/1891	Arthur Nikisch	Complete

SYMPHONY NO. 3

Freelance Orchestra (Boston)

11/21/1904	G. W. Chadwick	Complete

Boston Symphony Orchestra

10/19-20/1894	G. W. Chadwick	Complete (Premiere)
03/13-14/1914	Karl Muck	Complete
03/19/1914	Karl Muck	Complete
03/26/1914	Karl Muck	Complete

Chicago Symphony Orchestra		
01/08-09/1897	Theodore Thomas	Complete
01/03-04/1919	G. W. Chadwick	Complete
Detroit Symphony Orchestra		
04/22-24/1993	Neeme Järvi	Complete

SYMPHONIC SKETCHES

Freelance Orchestra (Boston)		
10/02/1903	G. W. Chadwick	"Noël" only
	(Worcester County Musical Association)	
03/23/1904	G. W. Chadwick	"Jubilee" and "Vagrom Ballad" only
	(Chickering production)	
11/21/1904	G. W. Chadwick	"Noël" and "Hobgoblin" only
	(Jordan Hall)	
Atlanta Symphony Orchestra		
06/13/1982	William Fred Scott	"Jubilee" only
12/11/1982	William Fred Scott	"Noël" only
06/22/1983	William Fred Scott	"Jubilee" only
12/03/1983	William Fred Scott	"Noël" only
12/29/1984	William Fred Scott	"Noël" only
06/21/1985	William Fred Scott	"Jubilee" only
10/05-06/1990	William Fred Scott	"Jubilee" only
Boston Symphony Orchestra		
02/7-8/1908	Karl Muck	Complete (Premiere)
Chicago Symphony Orchestra		
01/21-22/1910	G. W. Chadwick	Complete
12/22-23/1911	Frederick Stock	"Noël" only
12/28/1922	Frederick Stock	"Jubilee" only
12/22-23/1932	Frederick Stock	"Jubilee" and "Noël"
12/26/1944	Desire Defauw	"Noël" only
12/18/1967	Morton Gould	"Jubilee" only
Detroit Symphony Orchestra		
12/16/1961	Walter Poole	Complete
12/17/1963	Walter Poole	"Noël" only
04/23-26/1992	Neeme Järvi	"Jubilee" only
04/15-18/1993	Neeme Järvi	"Noël"only
Florida Philharmonic Orchestra		
07/10/1991	John Yaffé	"Jubilee" only

Houston Symphony Orchestra		
07/02/1981	R. Horwood	“Jubilee” only
Indianapolis Symphony Orchestra		
01/04/1939	Fabien Sevitzky	“Noël” only
02/09/1941	Charles O’Connell	“Jubilee” only
02/02/1944	Charles O’Connell	“Jubilee” only
11/20-21/1954	Fabien Sevitzky	“Jubilee” only
09/16/1976	Oleg Kovalenko	“Jubilee” only
07/03/1987	William H. Curry	“Jubilee” only
07/03/1987	William H. Curry	“Jubilee” only
Los Angeles Philharmonic		
04/26/1929	Artur Rodzinski	Complete
12/26/1929	Artur Rodzinski	“Jubilee” and “Noël”
08/19/1941	Howard Barlow	“Jubilee” only
09/02/1942	Edwin McArthur	“Jubilee” only
08/06-07/1943	Albert Coates	“Jubilee” only
Milwaukee Symphony Orchestra		
12/14/1961	Harry J. Brown	Complete
02/12-13/1977	James Paur	Complete
11/20, 23-25/1984	Lukas Foss	Complete
Minnesota Orchestra (Minneapolis Symphony Orchestra)		
01/03/1908	Emil Oberhoffer	Complete
02/16/1908	Emil Oberhoffer	“Jubilee” only
12/20/1908	Emil Oberhoffer	“Noël” only
03/21/1909	Emil Oberhoffer	“Jubilee” only
12/26/1909	Emil Oberhoffer	“Noël” only
12/25/1910	Emil Oberhoffer	“Noël” only
01/22/1911	Emil Oberhoffer	“Jubilee” only
12/21/1911	Emil Oberhoffer	“Noël” only
12/15/1912	Emil Oberhoffer	“Jubilee” only
02/13/1914	Emil Oberhoffer	“Jubilee” only
03/20/1914	Emil Oberhoffer	“Jubilee” only
12/24/1916	Emil Oberhoffer	“Noël” only
12/30/1917	Emil Oberhoffer	“Jubilee” only
03/22/1918	Emil Oberhoffer	“Jubilee” and “Noël”
12/22/1918	Emil Oberhoffer	“Noël” only
02/22/1920	Emil Oberhoffer	“Jubilee” only
12/25/1921	Engelbert Roentgen	“Noël” only
12/21/1924	unknown	“Noël” only

12/20/1935	Eugene Ormandy	"Noël" only
07/04/1984	Norman Leyden	"Jubilee" only
Philadelphia Orchestra		
12/24-26/1936	Eugene Ormandy	"Noël" only
12/29/1936	Eugene Ormandy	"Noël" only
12/19-20/1958	William Smith	"Noël" only
10/14/1959	William Smith	"Jubilee" only
10/27/1975	William Smith	"Jubilee" only
11/24/1975	William Smith	"Jubilee" only
12/11-13, 15-16/ 1975	Eugene Ormandy	"Jubilee" and "Noël"
11/25/1981	William Smith	"Jubilee" only
08/22/1985	Gunther Schuller	"Jubilee" only
07/09/1986	William Smith	"Jubilee" only
07/08/1987	William Smith	"Jubilee" only
Pittsburgh Symphony Orchestra		
12/05-07/1941	Fritz Reiner	Complete
Saint Louis Symphony		
11/09-10/1928	Emil Oberhoffer	"Jubilee" only
06/16/1991	D. Loebel	"Jubilee" only
03/18/1992	D. Loebel	"Jubilee" only
San Francisco Symphony		
01/23/1914	Henry Hadley	"Jubilee" only
07/04/1989	Andrew Massey	"Jubilee" only
07/20/1989	Andrew Massey	"Jubilee" only

SINFONIETTA

Freelance Orchestra (Boston)		
11/21/1904	G. W. Chadwick	Complete (Premiere)
Boston Symphony Orchestra		
02/11-12/1910	Max Fiedler	Complete
04/25-26/1930	Serge Koussevitzky	Complete
New York Symphony Orchestra		
01/02/1910	Walter Damrosch	Complete
St. Louis Symphony Orchestra		
12/16/1907	Max Zach	Complete

SUITE SYMPHONIQUE

Boston Symphony Orchestra		
04/13, 15/1911	G. W. Chadwick	Complete

Chicago Symphony Orchestra		
02/2-3/1912	Frederick Stock	Complete
Minnesota Orchestra (Minneapolis Symphony Orchestra)		
01/12/1912	Emil Oberhoffer	Complete
Philadelphia Orchestra (Philadelphia Symphony Orchestra)		
03/29/1911	G. W. Chadwick	Complete (Premiere)
San Francisco Symphony		
02/07/1913	Henry Hadley	Complete
Saint Louis Symphony Orchestra		
01/31/1913	Max Zach	Complete
02/01/1913	Max Zach	Complete

SELECTED DISCOGRAPHY

Chadwick, George Whitefield. *Symphonic Sketches*. Eastman-Rochester Orchestra, Howard Hanson, conductor. Mercury SR90018 (1956). Reissued 434 337-2 (1994).

———. *Sinfonietta in D Major*. American Arts Orchestra, Karl Krueger, conductor. Society for the Preservation of the American Musical Heritage, MIA-104. (1959).

———. Symphony No. 2 in B^b Major, Op. 21. Royal Philharmonic Orchestra, Karl Krueger, conductor. Society for the Preservation of the American Musical Heritage, MIA-134. (1967).

———. Symphony in F (No. 3). Royal Philharmonic Orchestra, Karl Krueger, conductor. Society for the Preservation of the American Musical Heritage, MIA-140. (1968).

———. Symphony No. 2 in B^b Major, Op. 21. Albany Symphony Orchestra, Julius Hegyi, conductor. New World Records, NW-339-2. (1986).

———. Symphony in F (No. 3). Detroit Symphony Orchestra, Neeme Järvi, conductor. Chandos 9253. (1994).

———. *Symphonic Sketches*. Detroit Symphony Orchestra, Neeme Järvi, conductor. Chandos 9334. (1995).

———. Symphony No. 2 in B^b Major, Op. 21. Detroit Symphony Orchestra, Neeme Järvi, conductor. Chandos 9334. (1995).

SELECTED BIBLIOGRAPHY

BOOKS AND ARTICLES

Baker's Biographical Dictionary of Musicians. Sixth edition, revised and edited by Nicolas Slonimsky. New York: Schirmer, 1978.

Beveridge, David. "Sophisticated Primitivism: The Significance of Primitivism in Dvořák's American Quartet." *Current Musicology* 24 (1977): 25–36.

Block, Adrienne Fried. "Dvořák, Beach and American Music." In *A Celebration of American Music: Words and Music in Honor of H. Wiley Hitchcock,* ed. Richard Crawford, R. Allen Lott, and Carol Oja, 256–280. Ann Arbor: University of Michigan Press, 1990.

Bomberger, E. Douglas. *The German Musical Training of American Students, 1850–1900*. Ph.D. Diss., University of Maryland, 1991.

Campbell, D. G. *George W. Chadwick: His Life and Works*. Ph.D. Diss., Eastman School of Music, Univ. of Rochester, 1957.

Chadwick, George Whitefield. "American Composers." In *History of American Music,* ed. by W. L. Hubbard, 1–15. Toledo: Irving Squire, 1908.

Chase, Gilbert. *The American Composer Speaks: A Historical Anthology, 1770–1965*. Baton Rouge: Louisiana State University Press, 1966.

Chase, Gilbert. *America's Music*. Revised 3rd edition. Urbana, Ill.: University of Illinois Press, 1987.

Chmaj, Betty E. "Fry versus Dwight: American Music's Debate Over Nationality." *American Music* 3/1 (Spring 1985): 63–85.

Clapham, John. "Dvořák on the American Scene." *19th-Century Music* 5/1 (Summer 1981), 16–23.

Clapham, John. "The Evolution of Dvořák's Symphony *From the New World.*" *Musical Quarterly* 44 (1958), 167–183.

Clarke, Garry E. *Essays on American Music*. Contributions in American History, no. 62. Westport, Conn.: Greenwood, 1977.

Crawford, Richard. "Musical Learning in Nineteenth-Century America." *American Music* 1/1 (Spring 1983): 1–11.

Culbertson, Evelyn Davis. "Arthur Farwell's Early Efforts on Behalf of American Music, 1889–1921." *American Music* 5/2 (Summer 1987): 156–175.

Dwight, John Sullivan. "Music in Boston." In *The Memorial History of Boston, including Suffolk County, Mass. 1630–1880.* Edited by J. Winsor. Boston: Ticknor, 1881.

Elson, Louis, C. *The History of American Music*. London: Macmillan, 1904.

Elson, Louis C. "George Whitefield Chadwick." *Musician* 10/12 (1916): 505.

Engel, Carl. "George W. Chadwick." *Musical Quarterly* 10 (1924): 438–457.

Everett, William Arlie. *The Symphonies of John Knowles Paine*. Master's Thesis, Southern Methodist University, 1986.

Fay, Amy. *More Letters of Amy Fay: The American Years, 1879–1916*. Selected and edited by Margaret William McCarthy. Detroit: Information Coordinators, 1986.

Foote, Arthur. *An Autobiography*. Norwood, Mass.: Plimpton, 1946.

Foote, Arthur. "A Bostonian Remembers." *Musical Quarterly* 23 (1937): 37–44.

Gilbert, Henry F. "The American Composer." *Musical Quarterly* 1/1 (1915): 169–180.

Goodrich, Alfred John. *Complete Musical Analysis*. Cincinnati: Church, 1889.

Hamm, Charles. *Music in the New World*. New York: Norton, 1983.

Hitchcock, H. Wiley. *Music in the United States: A Historical Introduction*. Englewood Cliffs, N.J.: Prentice-Hall, 1988.

Hitchcock, H. Wiley and Stanley Sadie, eds. *The New Grove Dictionary of American Music*. London: Macmillan, 1986. S.v. "Chadwick, George Whitefield," by Victor Fell Yellin and Steven Ledbetter.

Horowitz, Joseph. "Beach, Chadwick: New World Symphonists." *New York Times*. October 27, 1991, 25(H).

Howard, John Tasker. *Our American Music*. New York: Crowell, 1931.

Howe, M.A. DeWolfe. *The Boston Symphony Orchestra, 1881–1931*. Cambridge, Mass.: Riverside, 1931.

Howells, William Dean. *Suburban Sketches*. Boston: Houghton Mifflin, 1901.

Kearns, William K. *Horatio Parker, 1863–1919: His Life, Music, and Ideas*. Metuchen, N.J.: Scarecrow, 1990.

Kingman, Daniel. *American Music: A Panorama*. New York: Schirmer, 1979.

Krueger, Karl. *The Musical Heritage of the United States: the Unknown Portion*. New York: Society for the Preservation of the American Musical Heritage, Inc.: 1973.

Lang, Paul Henry. *One Hundred Years of Music in America*. New York: Schirmer, 1961.

Langley, A. L. "Chadwick and the New England Conservatory of Music." *Musical Quarterly* 21 (1935): 39–52.

LaRue, Jan. *Guidelines for Style Analysis*. New York: Norton, 1970.

Ledbetter, Steven. "George W. Chadwick: A Sourcebook" Ms [photocopy]. Spaulding Library, New England Conservatory of Music (Boston), 1983.

Levy, Alan Howard. *Musical Nationalism: American Composer's Search for Identity*. Westport, Conn.: Greenwood, 1983.

Levy, Alan Howard. "The Search for Identity in American Music, 1890–1920." *American Music* 2/2 (Summer 1984): 70–81.

Mason, Daniel G. *The Dilemma of American Music and Other Essays*. New York: Macmillan, 1928; reprint ed., Westport, Conn.: Greenwood, 1969.

Mason, Daniel G. *Tune In, America*. New York: Knopf, 1930.

Mason, Daniel G. *Music in My Time and Other Reminiscences*. New York: Macmillan, 1938; reprint ed., Westport, Conn.: Greenwood, 1970.

Mathews, W.S.B. "The American Composer and American Concert Programs." *The Musician* 8/6 (June 1903): 204.

Maust, W. R. *The Symphonies of Anthony Philip Heinrich Based on American Indian Themes*. Ph.D. Dissertation, Indiana University, 1973.

McKinley, Ann. "Music for the Dedication Ceremonies of the World's Columbian Exposition in Chicago, 1892." *American Music* 3/1 (Spring 1985): 42–51.

Mellers, Wilfred. *Music in a New Found Land*. New York: Knopf, 1965.

Moore, MacDonald Smith. *Yankee Blues: Musical Culture and American Identity*. Bloomington: Indiana University Press, 1985.

Morgan, Robert P. "Ives and Mahler: Mutual Responses at the End of an Era." *19th-Century Music* 2/1 (July 1978), 72–81.

Mussulman, Joseph A. *Music in the Cultured Generation: A Social History of Music in America, 1870–1900*. Evanston, Ill.: Northwestern University Press, 1971.

Nye, Russel Blaine. *Society and Culture in America, 1830–1860*. New York: Harper and Row, 1974.

Ostrander, Gilman. *American Civilization in the First Machine Age: 1890–1940*. New York: Harper and Row, 1970.

Potter, Hugh M. *False-Dawn: Paul Rosenfeld and Art Music in America, 1916–1946*. Ann Arbor: Published for the University of New Hampshire by Microfilms International, 1980.

Primmer, Brian. "Unity and Ensemble: Contrasting Ideals in Romantic Music." *19th-Century Music* 6/2 (Fall 1982): 97.

Ritter, Frederic Louis. *Music in America*. New York: Charles Scribner's Sons, 1900.

Rockwell, John. "Paine and Chadwick Return to Favor." *New York Times,* Sunday, January 15, 1989, H23.

Roman, Zoltan. *Gustav Mahler's American Years, 1907–1911: A Documentary History*. Stuyvesant, NY: Pendragon, 1989.

Rosenfeld, Paul. *An Hour with American Music*. Philadelphia: J. B. Lippincott, 1929.

Sablosky, Irving. *What They Heard: Music in America, 1852–1881, from the Pages of "Dwight's Journal of Music."* Baton Rouge: Louisiana State University Press, 1986.

Salomon, Roger B. "Realism as Disinheritance: Twain, Howells and James." *American Quarterly* 16/4 (Winter 1964): 531–544.

Schaun, George. *The Story of Music in America.* Annapolis: Greenberry, 1965.

Shanet, Howard. *Philharmonic: A History of New York's Orchestra.* Garden City, N.Y.: Doubleday, 1975.

Simpson, Anne Key. *Hard Trials: The Life and Music of Harry T. Burleigh.* Metuchen, N.J.: Scarecrow, 1990.

Tawa, Nicholas E. *The Coming of Age of American Art Music: New England's Classical Romanticists.* Westport, Conn.: Greenwood, 1991.

Tawa, Nicholas E. *Serenading the Reluctant Eagle: American Musical Life, 1925–1945.* New York: Schirmer, 1984.

Tawa, Nicholas E. *A Sound of Strangers: Musical Culture, Acculturation, and the Post-Civil War Ethnic American.* Metuchen, N.J.: Scarecrow, 1982.

Thomson, Virgil. *American Music Since 1910.* New York: Holt, Rinehart and Winston, 1971.

Tischler, Barbara L. *An American Music: The Search for an American Musical Identity.* New York: Oxford University Press, 1986.

Tischler, Barbara L. "One Hundred Percent Americanism and Music in Boston during World War II." *American Music* 4/2 (Summer 1986): 164–176.

Yellin, Victor, F. "Chadwick, American Realist." *Musical Quarterly* 61 (1975): 77–97.

Yellin, Victor F. *Chadwick, Yankee Composer.* Washington, D.C.: Smithsonian Institution Press, 1990.

Yellin, Victor, F. *The Life and Operatic Works of George W. Chadwick*. Ph.D. Diss., Harvard University, 1957.

Zuck, Barbara. *A History of Musical Americanism*. Ann Arbor: UMI Research Press, 1981.

MANUSCRIPT SCORES

Chadwick, George Whitefield. Symphony [No. 1] in C Major, Op. 5. 1881. Library of the New England Conservatory of Music, Boston, Mass.

———. Symphony No. 2 in B^b Major, Op. 21. 1883–5. Music Collection of the Library of Congress, Washington, D.C.

———. Symphony in F (No. 3). 1893–4. Music Collection of the Library of Congress, Washington, D.C.

———. *Symphonic Sketches*. 1895–1904. Music Collection of the Library of Congress, Washington, D.C.

———. *Sinfonietta in D Major* (Not located).

———. *Suite Symphonique in E^b Major* (Not located).

PUBLISHED SCORES

Chadwick, George Whitefield. Symphony No. 2 in B^b Major. Boston: Schmidt, 1888; reprint, New York: Da Capo, 1972.

———. Symphony in F (No. 3). Boston: Schmidt, 1896.

———. *Sinfonietta in D*. New York: Schirmer, 1906.

———. *Symphonic Sketches*. New York: Schirmer, 1907.

———. *Suite Symphonique in E^b Major*. Boston: Schmidt, 1911.

NEWSPAPERS

Boston Evening Transcript
Boston Globe
Boston Herald
Boston Journal
Boston Monitor
Boston Post
Buffalo (NY) *Express*
New York Sun
New York Times
Philadelphia Evening Bulletin
Philadelphia Inquirer

INDEX

Albany (NY) Symphony Orchestra, 201
American Art Journal, 60
Apollo Club, 195
Atlanta Symphony Orchestra, 196
Auber, Louis, 3

Bach, Johann Sebastian, 115, 157
Barlow, Howard, 197
Beethoven, Ludwig van, xvi, 16, 57, 65, 82
Berlioz, Hector, 3, 122
Beveridge, David, 42–43, 98
Bispham, David, 4
Bird, Arthur, 110
Bizet, Georges, 94, 121–22
Bomberger, E. Douglas, 2
Boston Evening Transcript, 75, 136
Boston Globe, 85, 113
Boston Herald, 54, 108, 132, 134
Boston Journal, 134
Boston Monitor, 135
Boston Post, 53, 134
Boston Symphony Orchestra, xv, 3, 51, 60–62, 83–84, 88–89, 107–8, 110, 114, 121, 123, 134, 140, 155, 167, 195–96, 198
Brahms, Johannes, 3, 5, 18, 22, 61–62, 64, 68, 77–78, 80–82, 85, 109–11, 119, 166–67
Bristow, George Frederick, xvi–xvii
Brown, Harry J., 197
Bruckner, Anton, 135–35
Buck, Dudley, 1
Buffalo (NY) Express, 84

Chabrier, Emmanuel, 3
Chadwick, George Whitefield: works, *Angel of Death,* 168; *Aphrodite,* 138, 168; *Cleopatra,* 168; *Columbian Ode,* 168; *Everywoman Waltz,* 89; *Melpomene,* 168, 176; *Miller's Daughter,* 168; *Phoenix Expirans,* 76, 168; *Pilgrim's Hymn,* 168; *Rip van Winkle,* 3, 8, 16, 36, 51, 56; *Sinfonietta,* 87, 116–37, 142, 146, 152, 155, 161, 163–65, 167–68, 198; *Suite Symphonique,* 87, 138–59, 161, 163–65, 167–69, 198; Symphonic Sketches, 87, 89–116, 119–20, 125, 129–30, 134–36, 138, 142, 146, 152, 156–57, 160, 163–69, 196; Symphony No. 1, 6, 8–33, 51, 54, 61, 83, 90, 161–63, 165–66, 195; Symphony No. 2, 7, 34–59, 61, 76, 83, 89, 91, 100, 160–63, 165–66, 169, 195; Symphony No. 3, 7, 60–87, 91, 114, 119, 120, 161, 162–63, 165–67, 169, 195; *Tabasco,* 168; *Tam O'Shanter,* 138; *Thalia,* 36; *Vikings Voyage,* 168

Chadwickian transition, 13–14, 27, 31, 40, 60, 63–66, 128, 141
Chicago Symphony Orchestra, 196, 199
Coates, Albert, 197
Converse, Frederick Shepherd, 4, 89, 161
Curry, William H., 197

Damrosch, Walter, 136–37, 158, 198
Davenport, Warren, 81–83
Debussy, Claude, 107, 119, 150, 156–58
Defauw, Desire, 196
Detroit Symphony Orchestra, 196, 201
Downes, Olin, 134–35, 169
Duveneck, Frank, 2
Dvořák, Antonin, xviii, 5, 42, 44, 49, 60–62, 75, 77–78, 82, 88, 106, 133, 159, 161, 167
Dwight's *Journal of Music,* 8, 58

Elgar, Edward, 86
Elson, Louis C., 79–81
Emerson, Ralph Waldo, 115
Emery, Stephen A., 1

Farwell, Arthur, 4, 111
Fiedler, Max, 136, 198
Florida Philharmonic Orchestra, 196
Foote, Arthur, 77
Foss, Lukas, 197
Franck, César, 2–3
Fry, William Henry, xvi–xvii

Gade, Neils, 56
Gericke, Wilhelm, 109
Gilbert, Henry F., 6
Gottschalk, Louis Moreau, 94
Gould, Morton, 196
Griffes, Charles Tomlinson, 119

Hadley, Henry, 198–99
Hale, Philip, 57, 76–79, 81–82, 114–15
Hanson, Howard, 201
Harvard Musical Association, xv, 3, 9, 12, 55–56, 195
Haupt, Karl August, 2
Hegyi, Julius, 201
Heinrich, Anthony Philip, xvi–xvii
Henry, O., 115
Henschel, George, 195
Hill, Edward Burlingame, 3–4
Houston Symphony Orchestra, 197

Indianapolis Symphony Orchestra, 197
d'Indy, Vincent, 132
Ives, Charles, 85

Jadassohn, Salomon, 2
Jarvi, Neeme, 196, 201

Koussevitzky, Serge, 198
Kovalenko, Oleg, 197
Krueger, Karl, 201

Leyden, Norman, 198
Loebel, D., 198
Loeffler, Charles Martin, 110
Los Angeles Symphony Orchestra, 197

MacDowell, Edward, 3, 111, 157, 169
Mahler, Gustav, 123
Mackenzie, Alexander, 77
Mascagni, Pietro, 111
Mason, Daniel Gregory, 4
Massenet, Jules, 111
Massey, Andrew, 198
Mathews, W(illiam). S(mythe). B(abcock)., 4, 58

McArthur, Edwin, 197
Mees, Arthur, 58
Mendelssohn, Felix, 5, 9, 16, 56, 80–81, 125, 137
Milwaukee Symphony Orchestra, 197
Minnesota Orchestra, 197, 199
Moscheles, Ignaz, 1
Mozart, Wolfgang Amadeus, 82
Muck, Karl, 112, 115, 135, 156, 195–96

National Conservatory of Music, 60–61, 77
National Federation of Music Clubs, 140, 156
New England Conservatory of Music, 1,3, 159
New York Philharmonic, xv–xvi
New York Sun, 136
New York Symphony Orchestra, 157, 198
New York Times, 157, 168
Nikisch, Arthur, 195

Oberhoffer, Emil, 197–99
O'Connell, Charles, 197
Ormandy, Eugene, 198

Paine, John Knowles, xvii, 5–6, 9, 12, 82, 91, 161
Parker, H(enry). T., 110–11, 113, 156–57
Parker, Horatio, 2, 4
Paur, Emil, 80, 83, 109
Paur, James, 197
pentatonic (pentatonicism), xviii, 42–44, 49, 61–62, 69, 90–91, 94, 98, 101, 106, 163
Petersiliea, Carlyle, 1
Philadelphia Inquirer, 154
Philadelphia Orchestra, 198–99
Pittsburgh Symphony Orchestra, 198
Presser, Theodore, 1
Primmer, Brian, 162–64
Puccini, Giacomo, 111, 156

Raff, Joachim, 77, 82
Reinecke, Carl, 1, 2, 5, 169
Reiner, Fritz, 198
Rheinberger, Josef, 169
Rodzinski, Artur, 197
Roentgen, Engelbert, 197
Royal Philharmonic Orchestra, 201

Saint Louis Symphony Orchestra, 198–99
Saint-Säens, Camille, 45
San Francisco Symphony Orchestra, 198–99
Schubert, Franz, xvi, 82
Schuller, Gunther, 198
Schumann, Robert, xvi, 5, 18, 20, 22, 82
Scott, William Fred, 196
Sevitzky, Fabien, 197
Shepherd, Arthur, 3
Sibelius, Jean, 111
Smith, William, 198
Still, William Grant, 4
Stock, Frederick, 140, 161, 196, 199
Strauss, Richard, 109, 114, 132
Strong, George Templeton, 110

Tawa, Nicholas, 6, 12
Thayer, Eugene, 1
Theodore Thomas Orchestra, 58, 140
Thomas, Theodore, xvi, 87, 109, 161, 196
Thoreau, Henry David, 115
Thurber, Jeannette, 61

Verdi, Giuseppe, 3
Villiers-Stanford, Charles, 77

Wagner, Richard, xvi, 9, 16, 38–39, 56, 109, 111
World's Columbian Exhibition (1893), 58, 112, 168
Whiting, George, 1
Whitman, Walt, 115

Yaffé, John, 196
Yellin, Victor Fell, 2, 87, 89–91, 160, 162

Zach, Max, 198–99
Zschörlich, Paul, 85

ABOUT THE AUTHOR

Bill F. Faucett (B.A., Ph.D., Florida State University; M.M. Southern Methodist University) specializes in American music research. His major areas of interest include the music of George Whitefield Chadwick, nineteenth-century American orchestral literature, and music in the Confederacy. In addition to papers written on these topics, Faucett is a contributor to the forthcoming edition of the definitive German-language music encyclopedia, *Die Musik in Geschichte und Gegenwart*. Other interests include early music and the music of Brahms. Faucett currently teaches in West Palm Beach, Florida.